Schools and Churches in American Democracy

Books by H. Leo Eddleman

Schools and Churches in American Democracy: In Defense of Public Schools

By Life or by Death: A Practical Commentary on Paul's Letter to the Philippians

Schools and Churches in American Democracy

IN DEFENSE OF PUBLIC SCHOOLS

H. Leo Eddleman, Ph.D.

Exposition Press   *Smithtown, New York*

Quotations from *A History of the United States,* by Norman A. Graeber, Gilbert C. Fite, and Phillip L. White, copyright 1970, are used with the permission of McGraw-Hill Book Company.

Quotations from *The Colony of Rhode Island,* by Robert N. Webb, copyright 1972; *The Colony of New York,* by David Goodnough, copyright 1973; *The Colony of Massachusetts,* by Alice Dickinson, copyright 1975; *The Colony of New Jersey,* by Corrine J. Naden, copyright 1974; and *The Colony of Pennsylvania,* by Emil Lengyel, copyright 1974, are used by permission of Franklin Watts, Inc., a subsidiary of Grolier Incorporated.

Quotations from *Baptists and the American Republic,* by Joseph Martin Dawson, copyright 1956 by Broadman Press, Nashville, Tenn., are used with permission.

FIRST EDITION. Originally published under the title *Hail Mary—Are You Heeding the Blessed Virgin: In Defense of Public Schools* and revised in 1983

© 1982 by H. Leo Eddleman

ISBN 0-682-40144-7

Printed in the United States of America

To
Honorable Glenn Archer LL.D.
First Executive Director
of AMERICANS UNITED
For Separation of Church and State
1948-1976
American, Patriot, and Statesman

Contents

Introduction

In 1776 over 3 million people lived in the original thirteen colonies and 22,000 were non-Protestant (p. 50 and p. 58, #10 herein). *The Democratic Experience* notes a population of 5,308,483 for the same segment in 1800. Dr. Thomas Bohenkotter (*A Concise History of the Catholic Church.* Garden City, New York: Doubleday & Company, p. 348) says that Father John Carroll (the brother of the Catholic signer of the Declaration of Independence—some say "cousin") had about 35,000 Roman Catholics in Maryland out of a total of 4,000,000 Americans. The *Encyclopaedia Britannica*, Vol. 15, p. 1018, gives no more than 25,000 Catholics out of 4,500,000. These percentages vary from .555 to .875 (over half of 1 percent).

Nations of government-financed religious schools have not fared well. Americans are wise to keep their public schools as they began.

Both Oliver Cromwell (England) and William Penn (America) attempted theocracies in the late seventeenth century. But Protestantism's love of Christ-ordained liberty (John 8:32) would not adjust to the authoritarianism necessary to sustain a theocracy. Roman Catholicism embodies both the political and the religious aspects of a theocracy: the Vatican State and the Roman Catholic church.

Most Americans feel education's best habitat is a democracy, conditioned by, supported by, and led by people in the spirit of excellent education for the majority. Catholic influence and Protestant shortsightedness may yet secure legislation for government aid to parochial schools regardless of religious affiliation. If this happens, it will be to accommodate a religion whose followers were hardly one-half to one percent of the population when great Americans wrote the Constitution. But tax-supported schools could pour innumerable youth into a nation whose education idealizes state-church union.

Charles Carroll, sole Catholic signer of the Declaration of Independence (J. M. Dawson, p. 9), favored the American Revolution without reservation, devoutly supported the Constitution with its "religious freedom guarantees," and even advocated an American-selected hierarchy with religion adjusted to the needs and ideals of a democratic nation (Anson Stokes and Leo Pfeffer, *Church and State in the United States*, p. 50ff.). We would owe a postmortem apology to that sole Catholic statesman who signed the Declaration of Independence and stood for the Constitution as it is, Charles Carroll, Esq.

An "American-selected hierarchy" (selected by Catholic Americans, of course) has what undesirable feature(s)?

1

A Hint from History

The Roman Empire determined the state and plight of more human beings than any previous national entity through her size and ingenious application of legal ideology. Since the time of the splitting of the Roman Empire (c. A.D. 365), the second capital having been located at Constantinople (a name clearly derived from Constantine himself), several lesser empires such as the Turkish, the German, the Dutch, and others have had considerable holdings overseas that they have used to make their home bases stronger.

Great Britain became a much more extensive and a better example of far-flung imperialism. She made serious effort to grade the status of the nations within the empire so as to supply incentive for economic, social, political, and other achievements that would contribute toward unity and mutual advantage.

The United States now is the most influential example of nationhood since Rome. Her strength and greatness are distinctive because they are derived from commerce, political ideology, and a measure of culture, instead of geographical expansion and political authoritarianism.

While some of the aforementioned empires were great, the United States just may have exceeded them all in worldwide ties and influence, including the Roman Empire. The great differentiating factor is United States abstinence from efforts at direct rulership or political control of other nations. She holds the freedom of all people to be inviolate both individually and collectively.

The influence of the United States had become evident long before the organization of the United Nations. The United Nations is thus far an effective continuation of the objectives of the former League of Nations (Geneva, Switzerland and The Hague).

What has precipitated the almost unique influence of the United States throughout the world?

The releasing of people from unjust restrictions, as in the case of Cuba's treatment by Spain up to and through 1898, the freeing of supposedly advanced and educated people, like those of Germany in 1917-18 and 1941-45 from dictatorial madness, almost savor of profound secular humanism as much as or more than of enlightened self-interest. The motivation of secular humanism could be accepted without question but for the unique religious origin, background, and history of the United States. Historians generally agree that this nation's origin and development show religion both at the grass roots and towering above all other strands of her life and development. James Truslow Adams' *The Epic of America* is a competent example (Garden City Books, 1931, esp. p. 18ff).

The social movements of the United States, the dynamism of her private enterprise, the personal motivation within smaller movements as well as in education, have resulted in a worldwide influence based largely on her commerce, which has penetrated much of the earth in varying degrees and in different places. As the skills and volume of the United States' assembly lines have reached new achievements in technological and industrial productivity, the American way has become "the desire of all nations" for many people. Many phases of her operation and success have reached global dimensions. If imitation is among the sincerest compliments, if combining resources and skills into the production of wealth and achievement for all men's well-being comprise major criteria of success, then the overseas envy of the United

States is cause for sympathy and not antipathy. Her affluence at home has not been detrimental to her influence abroad.

The Constitution of the United States equips the respective states and their individual citizens with almost unlimited liberty. This has long continued to be a primary cause of admiration to students of government at home and overseas, regardless of how acutely some sincere Americans assume that the Constitution has retarded progressive change for some. But United States citizens join others in refusing to claim perfection. The amazing wisdom of the framers of the Constitution has produced a practical *modus vivendi* for a variety of both religionists and secularists that continues to be an abiding source of wonderment to all.

The colossal United States military potential is but one facet of the nation's almost illimitable technology, lavish resources, and dynamic population, as World War II amply demonstrated.

Through her industrial prowess United States interests seem to be expanding in ever increasing swells throughout the world. The last two decades of the twentieth century are witnessing the promotion and expansion of her commerce into ever increasing profitable opportunities abroad. Her inclination toward tranquil and pacific processes of change may comprise the first prosperous effort in history by any nation to pursue worldwide activities with no territorial designs on those with whom she does business. Hardly a nation overseas exists that has not been profited, elevated, and encouraged by the spiritual example, morale, methodology, and possibly the ideology of the United States.

During and after World War I, the validity of European predictions that had been proliferating throughout the preceding century became increasingly evident: the United States' power and influence were spontaneously though gradually approaching worldwide dimensions.

After World War II the Russian and Chinese poles of opposite charges could have gradually gripped over half the globe in a state of international paralysis. The 1980 rapprochement of the United States with Old China possibly has done more to assure further years or decades of peace in our time than any political move on the international scene. Such power as a nation during peace, not to mention the strategic role which the United States played during the last two world wars, is awesome.

How will the United States ultimately employ this ever increasing strength? This is the urgent question of thinking men. If Russia had the same power, the question would be more urgent. Why? The question is far from academic to men who have an international perspective, of men who know the history of ancient Assyria and Babylon and of the powers that precipitated World Wars I and II.

Britain's thoughtful Thomas Huxley once philosophized that he was not overwhelmed by the United States' volume of achievement or vast natural resources per se. He realized that size does not assure greatness and extension of boundaries does not make a nation impregnable. His great concern was what was America going to do with her power and wealth. His question strikes a chord of sympathy in thoughtful Americans. Will America's leadership spawn another Genghis Khan, Napoleon, Kaiser Wilhelm, or Hitler?

Dictatorships with ambitions of world dimensions do exist. Some governments not only fail to develop a country's natural resources for the welfare of the people, they actually have designed plans and means for making miserable all citizens who dissent from the governmental line. Where will Americans focus their power and achievement? Huxley's question received at least partial answers immediately in the wake of World War II: for the first time in a major international crisis the world saw a demonstration of distinctly new national character as the United States proceeded to rehabilitate its erstwhile mortal enemies, Germany and Japan, economically. In a few years America's former enemies were among her chief competitors in world markets, which she had just set free again for all people. Not since the first two Christian centuries (up to A.D. 314, approximately) had any people collectively shown more compassion and spirit of goodwill toward all men than did the United States in the aftermath of World Wars I and II.

History, its wars and tensions, its tyrants and men of goodwill, require at least passing notice. What are the principles of national greatness? More properly, what are the criteria of ethnic superiority, with goodwill potentially focused on all in justice and helpfulness?

The only two distinctive factors the United States has contributed to the world's political philosophy are (1) a clearly defined juxtaposition of government and religion in their distinct spheres; and (2) an inclination to share her faith, life, and creature comforts with others. This does not necessarily result from innate goodness: her capitalism presupposes enlightened self-interest. Profit is in the pattern, but a willingness to keep more than the profit motive is there.

This has involved, among other things, a unique kind of religious liberty. The Founding Fathers worded the principles in the Constitution clearly: "Congress shall make no law respecting an establishment of religion . . ." This is not simply the freedom to belong to the church of one's choosing, though it includes that. It is a literal reaffirmation of the Edenic principle, which the Founding Fathers apparently understood to be an indispensable aspect of man's milieu, coming as it did from the book of Genesis and from common sense. Howsoever the Creator produced man originally, He made him as free to do wrong as to do right. The United States government is among the first authorities, since the original Edenic principle of freedom, that does not meddle with religion either to coerce against it or to compel identification with or participation in it.

The American way in the United States Constitution is diametrically the opposite in nature, method, and purpose to that of most European countries. The first formal American document, the Declaration of Independence, professes faith in God: "all men are created equal." This statement assumes a Creator and a responsible government, which should accord all citizens equal and just treatment on the basis of obligation to the Creator. But functionally and operationally the government neither supports nor espouses any interpretation of religion beyond this. Its posture toward religion is not secular but neutral and permissive. For purposes of doctrinal teaching and ecclesiastical forms, the government does not support or promote the tenets or programs of any specific church or religion: "Congress shall make no law respecting an establishment of religion . . ." This plain legal statement by the Founding Fathers forbids explicitly and by implication sects, religions, or churches to openly or subtly seek financial or political advantage.

The slightest modification in this posture on religion would be retrogression. The United States would become like the countries of the Middle Ages if it adopted the principles of government/ church relationships that have mired nations in indecision and unproductiveness for centuries.

The Founding Fathers who settled the original thirteen colonies were mostly of evangelical Christian background. Their moral and spiritual stamina bore the fruit of the refinement of their persecutions in Europe, which had become so unbearable that hazardous escape to the American wilderness was their fond hope. Yet these Americans finally composed a constitution whose only limitation for citizens is that the practice of faith or the lack of it shall not penalize or jeopardize the welfare or security of another in practicing his faith or the lack of it.

The spiritual ideals of the Founding Fathers have brought us much. Social progress has fructified beyond that of all nations. Spiritual and moral progress, as yet unfinished, may yet buttress the social and economic benefits constructively. With serious effort, proper balance, and the dignity of the ideal that the bell never tolls for only one, we might yet approximate the poet's ideal of

Caesar's hand and Plato's brain
The Lord Christ's heart and Shakespeare's strain.

Ralph Waldo Emerson

Spiritual and moral responsibility are in the foreground from the time the early pilgrims landed at Plymouth Rock. The mystical purpose of the United States' *raison d'etre* may appear in the sailing of Luther Rice on Monday, February 18, 1812 as a missionary to India. Adoniram Judson sailed for Burma in the same month for the same purpose. These early American believers seemed to exude a sense of divine destiny for the country from the earliest years of nationhood. Was a predictive statement by the Founder of the Christian faith (Matthew 24:14) in part revelatory of the basic cause of United States coming into being? These robust, aggressive minds, Judson and Rice, were aware of a well-defined, deeply innovating historical destiny with specific goals for America. Americans were taking the Gospel into the Orient. Since the time of Rice and Judson, over 110,000 missionaries have left America for other parts of the world as emissaries of Christianity. Is this a vital integrant of the unique liberty of the United States? Does the unique religious motivation and final constitutional structure in early American history play a primary role here? A brief review of colonial history may point to an answer in chapter four.

From the foregoing it appears that the greatest democracy in history had begun (in 1776) seeking independence and self-realization. In subsequent chapters it appears that the Christian faith played a major role. The original thirteen colonies were not naive and inexperienced regarding "church-state" union.

NINE OF THE ORIGINAL THIRTEEN COLONIES HAD "STATE CHURCHES" WITH VARYING DEGREES OF UNION (*see note on p. 58*). PROPOSED INCOME TAX DEDUCTION FOR RELIGIOUS SCHOOLS ARE ABOUT TO BE PRESENTED TO CONGRESS, AND WE URGENTLY NEED TO SCRUTINIZE THEM RIGIDLY.

Officials of one religion have been clamoring for this for decades. Others are beginning to show signs of joining them. With at least forty-two major sects and religions in the nation, how can they decide to whom to give income tax deductions (*de facto* federal "aid" to religion)—or to whom to deny them?

This issue may become a greater strain on American brotherhood than anything since the Civil War. The Constitution can stand it, can we? The Edenic principle in Genesis 1:3 gave man absolute religious liberty. He was as free to do wrong as he was to do right. The American Constitution has come near to approximating this freedom. Should it be kept or changed? Today America is experiencing a nationwide spiritual and moral decline. Conditions will be better. Even churches are in a decline but . . . "all things work together for good . . ." eventually.

2

Mary, the Mother of Jesus (Acts 1:14)

"There is a well known tendency of human thought to oscillate from one extreme to another. I think this tendency was exhibited in several points of what we call the Protestant Reformation. It appears to me that this has been the case as regards the position of the Protestants toward the mother of Jesus. The Romanists, we may say without uncharitableness, have come very near making her an object of worship. Their theologians make nice distinctions on the subject, but practically, for the mass, she is really an object of worship, a sort of goddess. The Protestant mind, starting back in horror . . . , has seemed to shrink sensitively away from ever saying a word or thinking for a moment about the mother of Jesus."[1]

"Now I say that the Protestant mind has reacted . . . But isn't it a pity that we should go to the opposite extreme as regards the mother of our Lord?"[2]

The birth of Jesus Christ was not supposed to take place if the only world we have is the natural order. If there is no spiritual order of being, it could not have happened. Biologically and scientifically such a phenomenon is contradictory. But spiritually, revelationally, and for the sake of man's ontological completeness, it, or something approaching its equivalence, was the only logical explanation of life, personality, society, and history. Culminating in ultimate redemption for men freely choosing it, Christ's mission puts reason in what some have called speculatively "the human experiment," and that is precisely where we come to know the most highly honored woman that ever lived, Mary, the mother of Jesus.

We shall scan first her distinctive qualities and view her reaction to matchless experience as major evidences and determinants of her character. Finally we shall endeavor to understand her chief legacy to humanity.

The role of Mary was unique: that any woman should claim to have given birth to a male child is itself claim to a miracle because of life, the gift of life. It is beyond man's ability to understand such a miracle. But for her to claim that this child was the result solely of a divine visitation, that she had had no physical contact with a man, is claiming the supernatural. The verb in "I know not a man" (Luke 1:34), denying relations with a man, is a verb form suggesting absolutely never. Conception in itself is an extraordinary phenomenon. But for Mary's claim to have been predicted by ancient prophets (Isa. 7:14; 9:6; Mic. 5:2) and later narrated as history by both a doctor (Luke 1:26-35) trained in the medical expertise and wisdom of his day (Col. 4:14) and by at least one businessman (Matt. 1:22-23) still does not place the claim scientifically beyond the natural tendency of man to question or try to refute it. But it does require thought equal to syllogistical reasoning or laboratory deduction.

For the One for whom Mary claimed supernatural conception to have died early (age thirty-three years and three or four months) at the hands of the state, with men around him saying the death He was dying was not that of a human (Luke 23:42; Mark 15:39), then for hundreds, who had known him well, to lay positive claims to seeing Him quite alive beginning three days after His death and risk their lives (in most cases being executed or mobbed to death from Jerusalem to Rome), culminated in millions believing Him to be alive today.

This helps elevate the accounts of the Virgin Birth in the direction of hard-core realistic history and not myth, cult, or legend. Millions who have since negotiated with Him for salvation and self-realization report their experience as a case of mind meeting Mind. It is logical and fitting and appears experientially to be what mind created by Infinitude is supposed to do.

A renewal of interest in Mary's greatness and spiritual power is long overdue. Besides, we want to know specifically what is her function and how we should relate to her. We want to identify the authority for such. She was the human channel through whom history's most Significant Personage made ingress into the world. If the only thing we know about her is that she was "Mary, the mother of Jesus," that would make her the most famous woman any of us know. But this lofty station and unsurpassed honor among women was not all easy fame and glory. Much of what she endured and suffered explains her extraordinary character.

Her first poignant hardship came on realizing that she, an unmarried young maiden (her exact age does not appear in the Bible), was to give birth to a child. The rigid Mosaic laws about adultery and pregnancy out of wedlock shock the modern mind (Deut. 22:21). Two factors sustained and strengthened Mary in what at best was a trying experience. The first was her unwavering confidence ever since Gabriel the angel first appeared and announced to her that she was to have a son of divine origin. Gabriel said on the visit of the annunciation: "Fear not, Mary . . . He shall be great, and shall be called the Son of the Most High: and the Lord God shall give unto Him the throne of David His father . . ." (Luke 1:30-32, Douay Version). To receive this communication directly from heaven through an angel of extraordinary rank from the Old Testament would give her confidence and sustain her regardless of what the public might say. Daniel is the only prophet to have predicted both the approximate dates of Christ's birth and death. This and similar assignments appear to give Gabriel elevated rank even for an angel (Dan. 9:21, 26).

Her second great heartache may have been the unceasing agony of concern over what people would be saying. Her never failing source of help was the sympathetic and understanding Joseph. At first he, "being a just man, and not willing publicly to expose her, was minded to put her away privately" (Matt. 1:19, Douay Version). If Joseph ever had any doubts about Mary's virginity, God concentrated on Joseph too the same supernatural communication that had reassured Mary. This crystallized and undergirded his own confidence.

THE TRUSTWORTHINESS OF THE DOCUMENTS

There may have been some "school of scandal" observations. Roman soldiers were prevalent; Jewish harlots were not unheard of. Roman soldiers jeopardized community youth and may have caused occasional moral tragedies. Joseph studiously rejected the rumors. He accepted supernatural communications arriving with the impact of the double confirmation to Mary and himself, each at a different time but chronologically near. The angel's communication to Joseph was a plain commandment: "But while he thought on these things, behold the angel of the Lord appeared to him in his sleep, saying: Joseph, son of David, fear not to take unto thee Mary thy wife, for that which is conceived in her, is of the Holy Ghost" (Matt. 1:20, Douay Version).

This account comes from a trustworthy document. It has been analyzed, criticized, and scrutinized by brilliant scholars for centuries. Two of the most knowledgeable Greek sages have spoken out vigorously as to the trustworthiness of these documents. Part of their evidence appears in chapter three. Much of it follows here at once, though the validation is A. T. Robertson agreeing with F. J. A. Hort: "With regard to the great bulk of the words of the New Testament, as of most other ancient writings, there is no variation or other ground of doubt, and therefore no room for textual criticism. Hort continues: 'The proportion of words virtually accepted on all hands as raised above doubt is very great; no less, on a rough computation, than seven-eighths of the whole. The remaining eighth, therefore, formed in great part by changes of order and other comparative trivialities, constitutes the whole area of criticism.' "[3]

Robertson adds on his own: "It is clear, therefore, that the *Textus Receptus* has preserved for us a substantially accurate text in spite of the long centuries preceding the age of printing when copying by hand was the only method of reproducing the

New Testament. But the case is even better than this presentation, for Hort continues: 'Recognizing to the full the duty of abstinence from peremptory decision in cases where the evidence leaves the judgment in suspense between two or more readings, we find that, setting aside differences of orthography, the words in our opinion still subject to doubt only make up about one sixtieth of the whole New Testament. In the second estimate, the proportion of comparatively trivial variations is beyond measure larger than in the former; so that the amount of what can in any sense be called substantial variation is but a small fraction of the whole residuary variation, and can hardly form more than a thousandth part of the entire text.' "[4]

The most dramatic evidence of the truth of the account of the Virgin Birth is its cumulative nature. These statements by Hort and Robertson, experts in Bible language, textual criticism, and manuscript history, are exciting and overwhelming. But to know that tough-minded, realistic Jews predicted many details of Christ's birth 700 to 1,000 years before it took place is equally convincing.

Three channels of Old Testament literature, wholly independent of each other, confirm and verify the New Testament narratives. First is the Septuagint (labeled LXX because, traditionally, an Egyptian king brought seventy Jews to Egypt about 285 B.C. to translate the Old Testament into the then rising Greek language). The Hebrew Old Testament contained the Virgin Birth prophecies, of course, and this is how they became firmly set in the Greek O.T. (LXX). The *Textus Receptus,* the Greek basis of the King James Version, including chiefly the Stephens text (1550) and the variant readings of the Elzevir text (1624, usually called E), never was without the Virgin Birth predictions.

The second line of Hebrew preservation that contains Virgin Birth prophecies is the Old Testament of the Massoretes (c. A.D. 960). This is the Hebrew Old Testament most widely used by Jews and Christians today. Its vowelization was invented around A.D. 960. Semitic languages originally had no written vowel forms as such.

The third confirmatory but wholly independent line of preservation of ancient Virgin Birth predictions is the Dead Sea Scroll in Hebrew, found in 1948. Isolated in a cave in large sealed jars and therefore independent of other texts for 2,000 years, it is surprisingly identical in content to the Septuagint and Massoretic texts, including Virgin Birth predictions. All combine in a vigorous testimony to the verisimilitude of the Virgin Birth narrative.

THE VIRGIN BIRTH AND PROPHECY

One of the most convincing evidences of a unique birth for the Coming One is that Isaiah (7:14) predicted it and its fruitage several times (Isa. 7:14; 9:6; 11:1; 42:1-4; 44:1-5; 49:1-6; 52:13-53:12) at least seven hundred years before it took place. Isaiah prophesied in some detail that the Coming One would be born of a virgin and that He would be called Immanuel, which means "God With Us" in Hebrew: "Therefore the Lord Himself shall give you a sign. Behold a virgin shall conceive, and bear a son, and his name shall be called Immanuel" (Isa. 7:14, Douay Version). In Isaiah 9:6 this Coming One would receive carefully chosen titles reserved for Deity only. Micah 5:2 foretold that He would be born in Bethlehem. Without this prophetic background, some would incline all the more to attribute the narratives of Jesus' supernatural conception and birth either to natural causes or to tradition comparable to Greek and Roman mythology.

Sign (Isa. 7:14a) is "portent," something unusual, either miraculous or unmiraculous. If it had been a woman and man, either married or out of wedlock, bringing a child into the world, there would have been nothing unusual about it except the moral issue. So both the context and the language require something extraordinary.

Anticipating doubt concerning the supernatural element, Luke, under inspiration, stated expressly: "Because no word shall be impossible with God" (Luke 1:37, Douay Version). "The Lord himself . . ." (Isa. 7:14b) emphasized this as God's doing by repeating the pronoun *himself*. The purpose of this emphasis was to expose the weak faith of King Ahaz. God had told him through

14

the prophet Isaiah (7:11) to ask for a sign: "Ask thee a sign of the Lord thy God, either unto the depth of hell, or unto the height above." God had told him to ask for a "sign" complicated ("either in the depth") or dramatic ("in the height above"). King Ahaz in affected reverence and humility replied, "I will not ask, and I will not tempt the Lord (Yahweh)" (Isa. 7:12, Douay Version). Then came the emphasis of "the Lord" initiating a preliminary sign and startling all that part of the world (7:22) by permitting Assyria to overrun it (8:6-8).

Isaiah 1:1-11:16 often goes under the heading "The Book of Immanuel," which means "With us God." Its prophecy of the Virgin Birth reaches a peak in 9:6, where Isaiah predicted the child would be called ". . . a wonder of a counsellor, a God of daring exploit, the Father of everlastingness, Prince of Peace" (lit. translation HLE). "For a child is born to us, and a son is given to us, and the government is upon his shoulder: and his name shall be called, Wonderful, Counsellor, God the Mighty, The Father of the world to come, The Prince of Peace" (Isa. 9:6, Douay Version). Isaiah's contemporaries, including King Ahaz, could assimilate this prediction of the Virgin Birth only by faith (7:9b), as could divine protection from King Rasin of Syria and King Romelia of Israel be seen only by faith as coming miraculously from their god Yahweh. So the coming of a baby whose greatness later would bring Him the titles of Deity would not be amenable to the natural mind apart from faith (Douay Version). The King James Version translates the titles "Wonderful, Counsellor, Mighty God, the everlasting Father, the Prince of Peace."

Syria and Israel were conspiring to attack King Ahaz (Douay Version) in Isaiah 7:1-2: "And it came to pass in the days of Ahaz the son of Joathan, the son of Ozias, King of Juda, that Razin king of Syria, and Phacee the son of Romelia king of Israel, came up to Jerusalem, to fight against it: but they could not prevail over it. And they told the house of David, saying: Syria hath rested upon Ephraim, and his heart was moved, and the heart of his people, as the trees of the woods are moved with the wind" (Isa. 7:2b, Douay Version). They had tried it unsuccessfully once and Ahaz's fright was unbounded, "as trees of the wood are moved with the wind." God would reassure King Ahaz through Isaiah, but Ahaz refused the comfort and challenge to ask for a "sign." Then God Himself initiated through Isaiah the prediction that the sign of the Virgin Birth would come ultimately betokening undreamed of security and prosperity for the Jews and all true believers through this Coming One (Immanuel).

"The virgin" (Isa. 7:14) has the definite article; this specificity emphasized that there is only one of the type: *ha-'Almah.* Some students have wondered why Isaiah did not use *bethulah,* the more common word for virgin. The answer is that it made the case of the Virgin Birth stronger because of well-known factors concerning Isaiah and his wife. They had two sons whose names were prophetic of Israel's destiny, making the case strong for the coming judgment of the Jews and for this ultimate triumph through One to be virgin born.

"Almah" is from the root *elem* which, with its derivatives such as *almah,* occurs in the Hebrew Old Testament only seven times. The references always point to objects, whether plant or animal, having eligibility for virginity. God gave Isaiah and his wife children: "Behold I and my children, whom the Lord hath given me for a sign, and for a wonder in Israel from the Lord of hosts, who dwelleth in Mount Sion" (Isa. 8:18, Douay Version).

The two sons by his wife symbolized temporary military crises; the Son to be born of the virgin would meet the permanent crisis of sin: his name was to be Immanuel. One of Isaiah's sons was She-ar-jash-ub ("a remnant shall return"). "And the Lord said to Isaiah: go forth to meet Ahaz, thou and Jasub thy son that is left, to the conduit of the upper pool, in the way of the fuller's field" (Isa. 7:3, Douay Version). The second son by his wife was Maher-sha-lal-hash-baz ("speed the spoil rush on the prey," in 8:1). "And I went to the prophetess and she conceived, and bore a son. And the Lord said to me: call his name, hasten to take away the spoils: make haste to take away the prey" (Isa. 8:1, Douay Version). Both names rebuke Ahaz for his unbelief by stressing the certainty of military defeat and exile for the Hebrews. Both occurred. Both names predicted military defeat.

Prophecy and revelation frequently operate behind a veil of

"divine incognito." A revelation is quite convincing to the recipient, but he can never put it in a test tube and prove it scientifically or mathematically to another. It is always by faith: "If you will not believe you shall not continue" (Isa. 7:9b, Douay Version). Isaiah (7:9) had just said: "And the head of Ephraim is Samaria, and the head of Samaria is the son of Romelia," showing God's knowledge of the problem alongside the king's fear and "unfaith." "If ye will not believe, surely ye shall not be established" (Isa. 7:9b, KJV). This shows that God has never changed: God said even in Genesis 15:6 (Douay Version): "Abram believed God, and it was imputed to him unto justice."

As far as Isaiah and the population at large knew empirically, many prophecies were fulfilled then and there, and those through Isaiah's own children, to some extent. Military defeat and exile came; but Isaiah, Ahaz, and all who read Isaiah's language (7:14; 9:6; 11-1; 52:13-53:12) knew that an age of "God with us" (Immanuel) was yet to come.

Troublous times would precede it, but it was still on the divine agenda. Little could they imagine that Messiah the Coming One would bring this people under judgment to a day of national fulfillment and to total spiritual redemption for all. They could or would not believe that His assignment would come and that it would depend seriously on the role of a first-century maiden bearing the name and character of a Jewish maiden of some 900 years earlier, the sister of the man who first led the Jews to nationhood, Miriam (root or stem of *Mary*), the sister of Moses (c. 1400 B.C.; Exodus 10-12, 15:21).

Why was it necessary that Christ be born of a virgin? Could he not have died and risen again anyhow? Could not salvation and eternal life have been secured without it? The logic of theology is not mystical at this point. It savors lavishly of the cosmic forensic concept and moves from law to grace by such a method as to avoid man's eternal security being tied with the human side of law. Christ's death completely satisfied the law once for all (Hebrews 10:8-10) when He offered His "body" as the sacrifice for our sin (predicted in Isa. 53:10).

Precisely at this point the meaning and the logical value of the Virgin Birth surfaces. *If Christ's death was to atone for man's sin, if His sufferings were to wipe the last vestige of guilt from man's soul and set him free* (Isa. 53:6), *the Lamb of God* (John 1:36) *which taketh away the sin of the world* (Revelation 12:11, 21:27) *must qualify to represent both God and man, both heaven and earth.* His saving work would need no supplement from any other source.

The Holy Spirit represented perfect Godhood because He is God. The Virgin Mary supplied the perfect manhood. If the Holy Spirit had been less than God or if Mary had been more than human (at the time or if she had been on a cosmic escalator of predeterminism gradually metamorphosing her into a state of "goddesshood"), then Christ's ATONING DEATH WAS IN VAIN.

To represent both sides equitably in reconciling, the Saviour had to originate in perfect Deity and in perfect manhood. Thus Christ was not half God and half man. Framers of creeds have been correct in saying that He was just as much God as if He were not man at all, as much man as if He had not been God at all. Only of Him can it be said that "in time He rested on the bosom of His mother without a father while in eternity He rested on the bosom of His Father without a mother, and that at the time of His birth He was as old as His Father and aeons older than His mother." (Dr. R. G. Lee).

Only such a One could "accomplish" (Luke 9:31) a totally efficacious death for sinful men (John 12:27). He is our hope and "the hope of Israel" (Acts 28:20). Again, if Mary had been more than human, or if the Holy Spirit had been less than God, Christ could not have qualified as mediator in dying for our sins.

THE VERY HUMAN BEHAVIOR OF GREAT HUMAN BEINGS

A quick death for Mary and no crucifixion for Christ would have resulted from an admission by Mary that Christ was not divinely conceived and that she was not a virgin at the time Jesus was conceived.

18

1.   First, premature death of the mother of Jesus would have been one of the most certain events in Jewish history if the evidence for the miraculous conception and birth of Jesus had not been strong beyond question. Mary and Joseph were espoused or betrothed (like our "engaged") at the time of Jesus' birth. (See Matt. 1:18; Luke 1:27, 2:5).

The law of Hebrew betrothal was very binding (Deut. 22:23-24). It was in effect a legal contract involving both parties. The only thing that could nullify the commitment of betrothal or espousal was adultery. The law required that death by execution of the guilty party follow nullification and exposure immediately. When two betrothed ones had been espoused about twelve months then the law required that the marriage be formalized. When the period of betrothal had been finished and the marriage was to be actuated and consummated, the woman was expected to be an absolute virgin.

If, by the methods and standards of their day, the damsel or wife-to-be was found not to be a virgin, she was to be stoned to death. The whole community could take part in stoning her. Customarily the one who had been sinned against would cast the traditional first stone (John 8:7).[5] The Mosaic code was harder on women than men. For example, it contained no provision for a woman to divorce a man. A man could divorce a woman easily, possibly with a note to her father, or "writing of divorcement" (Deut. 24:1; Matt. 5:31).

The treatment of a damsel who had lost her status of virginity was brutal. Stoning such a damsel in Deuteronomy 22:20-21 makes interesting if not unusual reading. The rigidity of these laws was not based on a single standard. They discriminated against women. The double standard appears with the usual cruelty in Deuteronomy 22:22. This might apply to a virgin damsel who had been betrothed "unto an husband" (the word *husband* is used sometimes during the period of betrothal, out of custom meaning the husband-to-be, the coming-husband, or the like as in Matthew 1:19). The man was not regarded strictly as the husband until after the twelve-month period of betrothal and the formal marriage (so in Matthew 1:19). This explains why Matthew 1:16

refers to Joseph as "the husband of Mary." In the genealogy his ultimate relation and station was and is properly husband.

The rigidity of Old Testament law on this subject goes beyond our imagination, particularly when held alongside modern laissez-faire promiscuity and contemporary breakdown in morals (according to sociologists, educators, and religious leaders). The strictness in Old Testament law is verifiable in Exodus, chapters 20 through 23, as well as in Deuteronomy, chapters 22 through 24. All of the laws are not negative nor do all of them deal with punishment or crime and the lowering of the standards of Israel. Some of them are very positive. "When a man hath lately taken a wife, he shall not go out to war, neither shall any public business be enjoined him, but he shall be free at home without fault, that for one year he may rejoice with his wife" (Deut. 24:5, Douay Version).

One thing appears certain in those portions of the Mosaic code that deal with betrothal, marriage, pregnancy out of wedlock, and the like. If God had not already dealt with Mary supernaturally, as the Bible claims, and if she could not account for her pregnancy by the Holy Spirit (Matt. 1:20; Luke 1:35), her death by stoning would have been sure and swift. Though some of her relatives may have tried sympathetically to shield her, such an untruth would never have let her raise her child peaceably and shamelessly as she did in Nazareth (Luke 2:48-52).

If Jesus had not been conceived by the Holy Spirit in the supernatural manner described in Matthew, chapters 1-2, and Luke, chapters 1-2, Mary would have died early and cruelly by stoning. Her yet-to-be-born baby almost certainly would have died with her. If Christ were not supernaturally conceived, almost certainly his mother would have died before He was born.

Inasmuch as all Bible evidence confirms that Mary gave birth to Christ while Mary and Joseph were still engaged (espoused, not married), it is certain that Jesus' birth came during the year of that contract of espousal or betrothal. Since this contract could be abrogated only by adultery, the inflexible law of Israel would have been invoked and death by stoning would have ensued inexorably.

The law was more cruel than what we read on the surface: the officiating priest would examine the accused one, he would hear the evidence from others involved, and then he would issue the sentence of condemnation. Some traditions maintain the one sinned against (as in the case of Joseph here) was the one who should cast "the first stone" in putting the woman to death. All the community were privileged to participate. Dr. Harry Rimmer, in *The Magnificence of Jesus,* states that "The exact wording of the basic law in this case was as follows: 'If a virgin espoused to a man is found to be with child, he shall denounce her before the council, and they shall stone her with stones til she dies; and thus shall ye put out sin from among the people.' "[6]

Mary knew the law. She knew the Old Testament well. In her incomparable Magnificat in Luke 1:46-55, she revealed a broad and deep knowledge of Old Testament Scripture. Therefore she would know also of the certain death for a betrothed woman who became pregnant out of wedlock. What did she do?

As soon as she found herself expecting a child, she went straight to her cousin Elizabeth and told her all about her shocking condition. Who was Elizabeth? The wife of Zacharias, the officiating priest of the temple at the time. He would be the person responsible for pronouncing sentence upon Mary. He would assign the time and place of execution, and his official word would be the signal for initiating and consummating the execution of the guilty party.

So according to the laws of the Pentateuch, which Jews strictly applied especially during the first century, and according to all known principles of human behavior, the evidence of the Bible accounts of the Virgin Birth are psychologically convincing. If Mary were pregnant out of wedlock by a Roman soldier, she would not have told anybody as long as she could possibly avoid doing so. Least of all would Mary have run to Elizabeth, the wife of the officiating priest (who would be responsible for her execution) and tell her that she was pregnant, as she did in Luke 1:37-41.

Elizabeth, the wife of the officiating high priest, instead of being shocked and running to report her to her husband, immediately told her of her own pregnancy and John the Baptist's near arrival! Elizabeth then issued the great blessing that was expected for the woman divinely chosen as mother of Messiah: "Blessed art thou among women and blessed is the fruit of thy womb" (Luke 1:42, Douay Version).

Instead of telling Elizabeth of the official priestly family, instead of sharing the information with anybody, if Mary had been pregnant by a man on this earth, whether Roman soldier or a Jewish roustabout, she would have kept it a secret as long as possible and then would have fled into obscurity until her child were delivered. Numerous alternatives would have been available in preference to sharing such a fabricated story as being the divinely visited mother of Messiah-to-be, if indeed such had not been the literal and unimpeachable fact as validated supernaturally to Elizabeth, Zacharias, the shepherds, and others (Luke 1:18-35, 45-48; Matt. 1:18-2:15).

Mary would have died the death of a felon, the death of a woman who was bringing shame on the state of Israel while posing as God's "Exhibit A" among the chosen people. The rigid law of execution by stoning (Deut. 22:23-24) was the nationally proscribed method of dealing with a citizen who lowered the moral standards of the nation.

Even if Mary could have kept the secret and then fled into the mountains, even if she could have resorted to some radical measure such as self-annihilation, the narratives of the dependable historians like Matthew and Luke are such as to justify the accounts of the Virgin Birth with many details involving many different characters. It is highly unlikely, if not absolutely impossible, that so many people could have had this information and kept it a secret were it not that the account as Mary related it was convincing and absolutely true.

Her account, if it seems extraordinary (and who would evaluate a virgin birth otherwise?), was matched by similar but not nearly as radical accounts, such as that of Elizabeth in her advanced years expecting a baby which had reacted suddenly upon the arrival of Mary in the room (Luke 1:41). The advanced years of Zacharias likewise ought to be brought into the picture (Luke

1:18-22; 57-64). Others unnamed would have been involved. It is unthinkable that the accounts contain any falsehood about how Mary came to be pregnant (Luke 1:39). Lamentable it is that so many Hebrews have failed to identify the account of this first coming of Messiah in the first three chapters of both Matthew and Luke.

The enemies of Christ, even they, in a heated discussion including some suggestive accusations about Christ being an illegitimate child, exclaimed shortly before His crucifixion, "When Christ cometh, shall He do more miracles, than these which this man doth?" (John 7:31, Douay Version). They were pointing out Christ's record of miraculous doings, which no conceivable Messiah in the future could exceed.

2.   The demeanor of Mary at the cross, the second feature in the biblical accounts, stands out as either a sharp indictment or an incomparable commendation of Mary. If Jesus had not been divinely conceived and virgin born, Mary could have, should have, and almost certainly would have stopped the crucifixion. But Mary was silent all the way through the six hours of the agonizing dying which Jesus "accomplished" (Luke 9:31) on the cross. This was what He had come to do and He set Himself to execute it with the courage and finesse of genuine manhood combined with creative Godhood (John 12:27; Luke 9:31; Isa. 53:3, 10-12; Zech. 12:10).

The mother of a baby ordinarily would do anything to protect her first born; she would aid it lavishly through life, and would derive her greatest sense of fulfillment in contributing to the final well-being and success of her child. For a mother to do otherwise, as sociologists have observed, probably indicates she has fallen to such a low state morally that only fleshly desires and physical subsistence can motivate her anymore.

Mary was not this kind of woman, according to all the evidence available. In her deeply spiritual and idealistic Magnificat in Luke 1:46-55, her rich knowledge of Hebrew ideals and Scripture show her at the highest level of womanhood.[7]

Yet Mary witnessed the sufferings and unfair treatment of her son on the day of His crucifixion. She was aware of the arrest of

Jesus the night before; she followed Him together with the others as far as she could penetrate near to the Praetorium hall (Mark 15:40; John 19:25). Since so many people were there, some of them nondescript (like the maids who all but badgered Simon Peter about his being one of the disciples of Jesus, Mark 14:66-72), Mary would have had no difficulty witnessing the smitings on the cheek, the mockery of the purple robe thrown on Christ as the symbol of mock royalty, and the other ignominies which the soldiers (with the permission of Pilate, apparently) heaped upon Christ (Mark 15:17-20).

During the crucifixion of Christ, at which His sufferings reached their peak, Mark wrote, "There were also women looking on afar off: among whom was Mary Magdalene, and Mary the mother of James the less and of Joses, and Salome; (40) (who also, when he was in Galilee, followed him, and ministered unto him;) and many other women which came up with him unto Jerusalem" (Mark 15:40-41).

John added, concerning this phase of the scene, "Now there stood by the cross of Jesus his mother, and his mother's sister, Mary the wife of Cleophas, and Mary Magdalene" (John 19:25). Since he mentioned Mary Magdalene, it can be taken for granted that "Mary the mother of Jesus" ("Jesus his mother" in John 19:23) was present in the group to which Mark referred in Mark 15:40.

The reason Mark did not repeat the name of Mary the mother of Jesus is twofold: first, his primary emphasis was to show that a faithful group of women who had "followed him" when "he was in Galilee" even followed to the deathly end and "many other women" from other parts of the country. To have called the name "Mary the mother of Jesus" would have detracted from Mark's purpose here. Second, Mark assumed with others that Mary the mother of Jesus was present with this group at the crucifixion of her son. Of all the people who would not be absent at this time, that was the mother of Jesus. So Mary the mother of Jesus had apparently followed from the time of mockings around the Praetorium hall all the way to the cross. She tread the Via Dolorosa in more ways than one!

She could have stopped the crucifixion at any time. How? As His mother she could have stepped forward, explained to the high priest or the military official in charge of the actual crucifixion, and identified the human father of Jesus, if such there had been!

"Stop that farce! Have done with that physical tormenting," a mother, a true mother would have exclaimed. Mary could have said it convincingly, if it had been true, "I'll tell you who his father was. With shame I confess that through an affair with a Roman soldier, this man was born. Stop his crucifixion and do it now!"

But there is no record of such an explanation on the part of Mary. Why? Because, of all people, she knew how He was conceived and born. The great events of the annunciation by the angel that she was to give birth to such a child, his precocious demeanor at the age of twelve when they made the journey to the temple, the many other things about this unique child later growing into manhood, the unique response of this son at the wedding in Cana of Galilee when he turned six firkins (approximately 42½ gallons) of ordinary water into good wine, all confirmed to her precisely who was hanging on that cross. She who had been so noble as to submit to this very typical assignment early in life, would not in later life go back on her son and betray Him in His divinely devised, providentially prepared, God-assigned function of dying for man's sin (Rev. 13:8).

Does not the role of Mary, a Jewish maiden (the virgin mother of Christ in the accounts of Matthew 1-3 and Luke 1-3), supersede the fictitious and apocryphal events that have appeared in literature intermittently? The tradition of Mary's assumption (to heaven without dying?), as it appears beginning on p. 34 herein, suffices to cause one to recoil at the thought of mixing Roman or Greek mythology with education as a primary strand in the authoritarianism that prevails in many schools. Those apocryphal narratives are interesting, but they elevate her to the rank of "queen" of heaven.

Notes

1. John A. Broadus, *Sermons and Addresses,* Fleming Revell, New York, 12 Bible House, Astor Place, Anal, Sept. '57, J.W.C. p. 124.

2. Ibid., p. 126.

3. A. T. Robertson, *An Introduction to the Textual Criticism of the New Testament,* Sunday School Board of S.B.C., Nashville, Tennessee, p. 21.

4. Loc. cit.

5. Harry Rimmer, *The Magnificence of Jesus,* Wm. B. Eerdmans Publishing Company, Grand Rapids, Michigan, 1947, pgs. 113-128.

6. Ibid., p. 114.

7. Ibid., p. 113-128.

3

Mary beyond Scripture

The most intriguing paradox of western religions is the Mary of the Bible and the Mary of subsequent cult and myth.

The Bible is the oldest literature on the Virgin Birth, the mission of Christ, and the role of Mary. But again, can we depend on the ancient original source? In the interests of fair-mindedness and objectivity, the real conflict in the textual criticism of the New Testament involves an infinitesimally small portion. Only a "thousandth part of the entire text"[1] leaves any question at all in the New Testament.

The trustworthiness of the records of Scripture is more strongly confirmed than perhaps any other document of antiquity. Fortunately the original information and primary sources on Mary appear in Matthew, Mark (6:1-5), Luke, and John.

The fascinating information about the blessed Virgin coming to us from other sources will be all the more meaningful if we apply the same tests of credibility in assessing all sources.

FACT, LEGEND, MYTH, AND CULT

The aura of sanctity in which Roman Catholics hold Mary shows reverence seldom equalled. Even those who do not follow the devotional suggestions and theological nuances can learn much.

Devotion to and worship of Mary has evolved from fact, legend, myth, and cult. The embellishment from literature, music, painting and the fine arts in general is prolific.

Myth is sometimes firmly ensconced in history. This does not mean necessarily that it has rootage in history. It may have originated in imagination or in emotion. But one way or another it got into history and to many, at least, it is now history.

> *cult*   A system of worship of a deity; as, the cult of Apollo, hence: a. the rites of a religion. b. great devotion to some person, idea, or thing, esp. such devotion viewed as an intellectual fad.
>
> *legend*   Any story coming down from the past, esp. one popularly taken as historical though not verifiable.
>
> *myth*   A story, the origin of which is forgotten, ostensibly historical but usually such as to explain some practice, belief, institution, or natural phenomenon. Myths are especially associated with religious rites and beliefs.[2]

Alone of All Her Sex[3] comprises so replete and studious a picture of the development of Mary in the contemporary thinking and theological convictions of many that one profoundly regrets the lack of space for reviewing the entire volume.

Authoress Marina Warner presents her material in five major parts which are Virgin, Queen, Bride, Mother, and Intercessor. This method and order help both the analytical mind and the worshipful heart.

In the prologue[4] Claude Levi-Strauss in effect makes a realistic claim that man does not and cannot have knowledge of the original faith and traditions whose seminal origins stem from a remote era of history. But for the now in which we live, we can assert confidently that our behavioral patterns, presumably spiritual and even theological, do not result from the impulses and feelings generated by our present milieu. People do not respond socially as social beings altogether but partially according to their own individual psychological and spiritual patterns. The individual reacts and responds to some degree along his individual patterns within the framework of the authority of his environmental or institutional ties. Every individual is so conditioned. At the inception his response is triggered by gregarious factors or how others seem to be responding in this repetitive response; this creates inner tendencies that become spontaneous and even sentimental unless vigorous thought or environmental factors eliminate the sentimental satisfaction and its dubious sense of security.

Although the remote past origins of cult and myth often elude us, we can survey the clearly indentifiable origins and trends of basic thought patterns on this subject as well as the influences of social and liturgical forms of ancient European and Roman sources.

Logically, if grounds and patterns of worship of female deities are well established in Roman history prior to and outside the Christian revelation and churches, they help trace tangential strands in worship of female deities that may converge on Mary. Worshippers of these goddesses could have readily attached themselves to the popular and growing Christian enterprise.[5] This could be true equally of other aspects of religion unless empirical evidence, such as that of the apostles on the resurrection of Christ, abounds to the satisfaction of analytical minds.

The increase in popularity of the original Christian movement and its pristine purity evoked prolific persecution. It did not yield ordinarily to the vigorous appeal of the liturgy of worship of goddesses. Early Christianity had a spontaneous tendency to recoil from the carnality that was repulsively prevalent in the Greek and Roman empires at certain times and places. The cult of Mary generally appears only with a high standard for all.

Some may have become adherents to the female goddess that had prevailed in the East because the Christianity nearest them comprised less vigorous rivulets of Christian life. They failed to experience the zest, momentum, and inspiration typical, for example, of the first gentile church (Acts 11:1-26).

Converts to the Christian way in Antioch lived near temples that had practices comparable to those of Ephesian and Corinthian temples. This particular expression of religion in the Roman Empire readily displays similar trends prevalent in Asia Minor and in the East in general. Some ancient literature, rites, theological aberrations from historical Christianity, and some customs in modern Italy suggest the development of Mariology as a belated integrant into Italy's state, or official, religion. The theology of the supreme mother of the Roman pantheon[6] (*pan* = all and *theōn* = gods) was prevalent. Ferguson's *The Religions of the Roman Empire* has the distinct advantage over most kindred volumes of substantiating its material by considerable evidence from archeological finds in addition to literary sources. Thus a trend toward an eclectic including female goddesses would quickly gravitate toward Mary. Further reasons based on the broader spectrum of natural life, trends, and needs appear below.

I. Mary the Virgin

In *Mary in the Gospels* (ch. one, pp. 3-24), Paul's emphasis in Galatians 4:4 that Jesus was "made of a woman" (Douay Version) shows the urgency of Christ being both totally human as well as the son of God in a unique sense. *Son of* is a Hebrew idiom denoting the absolute nature of an object or person. The Christ must be fully divine and fully human. To reconcile man and God, Christ must represent them both equitably. Thus He was also "son of man," a title appearing more frequently than "son of God" (Matt. 14:33). He was not part God and part man but all God and all man according to creedal suggestions.

The volume states candidly (p. 19) that neither the concept of Mary's perpetual virginity nor her being assumed directly into heaven appear in the Bible. Scripture, the original literary source of all information on Christ and Mary, carries much Mariology but no hint of continued virginity or immaculate conception.

Matthew claimed Mary's absolute virginity prior to her conceiving and giving birth to Christ (Matt. 1:8 and 20), and then he vigorously affirmed normal wifehood for her afterward: "And Joseph . . . did as the angel of the Lord had commanded him, and took unto him his wife . . . And he knew her not till she brought forth her firstborn son" (Matt. 1:24-25, Douay Version). *Knew* or *know* is the regular Scripture word or idiom for conjugal relations.

Thus if language means anything, this excellent Catholic version of the Bible says that the Virgin Mary supplied Christ with absolute humanity and shortly afterward became a normal wife to Joseph as a normal human herself. The four named brothers of Christ and reference to two or more sisters (Matt. 13:55-56; Mark 6:3) likely would have had some explanation had not the children been Mary's and Joseph's by the normal husband-wife process, in these Bible contexts. The suggestion of their being Joseph's children by a former marriage supports perpetual virginity. But this is not needed.

Mary could and did supply Christ's perfect humanity just as easily without perpetual virginity. Was it not fairer for Mary that her husband for the other children (half brothers and sisters) be as pure as she was? Why be solicitous for the prestige and privilege of virginity for one member of this select family and then deny them to others?

The volume refers to "eyewitnesses" in Luke 1:2 (p. 17—all citations in this chapter are from *Alone of All Her Sex* unless otherwise noted) as possible evidence that Luke heard his narrative of the birth of Jesus from none other than the Virgin Mother. Paul's two-year imprisonment in Caesarea has been long held as appropriate and ample time for Luke to visit Nazareth, Jerusalem, and Bethlehem to interview Mary and others. Luke's account of the Virgin Birth, accordingly, is more tender, intimate, and replete. See the first two pages of this chapter for the trustworthiness of the Bible. Compare it with the evidence for myth, cultism, and ecclesiastical authoritarianism. Luke's case for Jesus' Virgin Birth is as strong as Matthew's (Luke 1:26-35; 2:7-32, contravening p. 21).

Luke's nativity narratives are the Bible's place for the indispensable truths together with the basic mystique of Mary. Luke 1:1-2:52 is possibly the sole Scripture where Mary is truly at the center of things. This is because at the birth of Christ her role peaked naturally. She did what God had ordained her to do: she supplied perfect humanity to Christ.

In Philippians 2:5-11 on Jesus' Humiliation and Exaltation, neither Mary nor Peter nor any other creature is in the limelight.

Redemption and restoration came through Christ alone. Salvation, comfort, and intercession are His alone to give. That Mary the Blessed Virgin should have these qualities in eternity we naturally are prone to expect, or even yearn for, because of what motherhood in its femininity has meant to us in this life.

It is difficult to conceive of a supreme Being wholly self-contained yet absolutely independent of gender. But the God of Abraham, Isaac, and Jacob had these refined qualities in eternity tempered perfectly with compassion (Deut. 32:11). This was long before creation saw the concept of aggressive males and submissive females in His creatures.

Of all the several factors that the Omniscient Christ said would not continue in functional reality beyond the resurrection, the distinction between male and female is one of them (Matt. 12:24, Douay Version). Islam is the only religion whose holy writings seem to say otherwise. Islamic theology of a "holy war" explains this adequately.

Concerning Jesus' boyhood, one apocryphal source says He struck dead a lad for meddling with mud and waterway buildings. He adjusted the dimensions of planks Joseph had cut too short, but He would not submit to Joseph's "paternal" control over Him. Jesus brought immediate death to a meddler in his playing but only struck down a lad who hit Him (p. 29).

The Acts of Thomas (also apocryphal) hint that the Holy Spirit is the female originator of Mary (p. 38). This type of Christology is hardly consonant with the authoritativeness of Scripture, in either the Douay Version or the King James Version.

Jesus was a boy wonder worker (p. 29). But Scripture mentions only one appearance between babyhood and age thirty (Luke 2:41-52). It was germane solely to His saving mission.

Apocryphal James (p. 26-33) recognizes the readiness of both the Orient and Europe for the concept of the Mother of God. It also pictures Joachin, Mary's father, as a man of affluence who gave one-third of his wealth each year to the poor, a second third to the support of the temple, and kept only one-third for himself. The high priest on one occasion punished him for having no children; this was evidence of God's being displeased. Thus hurt, Joachin ran off to the wilderness for forty days of penitence, the dubious book claims. Anna, grieving, saw a cluster of baby birds in a nest, which made her sorrow more bitter. While she was crying God sent an angel to assure her that a child would be born to her. The same message arrived to Joachin in his desert recluse. This imaginary moment apparently has long been an *objet d'art*.

The Second Eve (pp. 50-67) reaffirms that the woman who gives birth to a Deity must be of absolute virginity. Protestant and Catholic Christendom join in holding this as a *sine qua non* in Christ's qualifications as Redeemer, held tenaciously by the early church also.

Affirming that the curse of death entered the race by way of Eve, the distinctive conditions of life have returned to mankind through Mary: sin and death entered by Eve, life and hope by Mary (p. 54).

Evidence found in Mount Sinai tends to support the following: Christ, immediately after his resurrection, appears before two good women and one of them is identified by two letters that comprise the historical mark of identity for Mary the mother of Jesus throughout the Byzantine areas of influence (p. 230). The author indicates (p. 231) that the Lord, as evidence of his being genuine in his son relationship to His mother, must have extended some such gesture to her that was not inferior to that extended to Mary Magdalene. In some dramatic productions, the Lord actually appeared to Mary his mother ere the guards at the tomb had awakened from sleep! But Jesus' mother was the only one who needed no resurrection appearance. Only she knew really! Origen had long before maintained that Mary Magdalene was a most improper person to be the first one to have seen the Lord on the morning of the resurrection. But whose prerogative and sovereignty decide what order of Jesus' appearances is more cogent for saving humanity? Were resurrection appearances based on sentiment, theology, or on human-family priorities?

The elaborate striving on this issue apparently stems from the desire to find some evidence that Jesus did appear to Mary His mother and not to Mary Magdalene only. Mary Magdalene was among the first, possibly the very first, to believe Christ to be alive after his crucifixion. "The other Mary" in Matthew 27:61 and 28:1 seems to be identical with "Mary the mother of James and Joses" in Matthew 27:56. That Jesus' mother did not have to be convinced is self-evident. What she knew about His conception and birth made resurrection "proof" superfluous for her. Desire for a female goddess of prestige no less than her of the Roman Pantheon just would not be content with a pure but human mother for Jesus.

In the area of influence of the church in the East, particularly in those sections where the tradition persists that Mary raised Joseph's children (born to him by a previous wife), this construction of events was more acceptable (See Matthew 13:54 and Luke 4:16). Even Chrysostom joined others in this interpretation. Chrysostom supposedly advocated that it was proper that the Lord had manifested Himself in His glorified body unto Mary His own mother, is the claim.

The reason Mary the Mother of Jesus was not at the tomb (p. 231) was simply that she had no need for it as did others. She was fully aware of what was going to transpire. This argument is positive and easiest of all to consider because it is consonant with the biblical fact of Mary's absolute certainty that her son was the unique Son of God. Mary knew the divine project to which she was contributing and, woman of faith and spiritual thought (Luke 12:19) that she was, she did not whimper for intermittent confirmations. Those of Europe seem to have taken the view of ecclesiastics of the East; it fit their pantheon.

In concluding a summary of the educative value of an extraordinary volume, we converge on four remaining major subjects: they are (1) Mary's assumption (as queen?); (2) Whether Mary is officially, informally, or in any real sense filling a role of queen in redemption in the next world (See ch. 7, Maria Regina); (3) Why Christ never appeared to Mary after His Resurrection as He did to Mary Magdalene; and (4) Is Mary an Intercessor?

II. Mary as Queen

A record of the death of Mary does not appear in the Bible (ch. six, pp. 81-102). This silence conduced toward speculation. It is not a denigration of Scripture even though the solicitous concern for Mary is finely wrought.

August 15 (p. 81) supposedly marks the time of Mary's passing, as enunciated in the days of Emperor Maurice about A.D. 600 in the eastern part of the Empire. About a half century later the same proclamation was duly noted in the western part.

Narratives as to miraculous events that transpired at the time of Mary's demise almost caused the world to rock and reel. Note that at Christ's death a worldwide darkness came at high noon (Matthew 27:34), a shocking but temporary resurrection occurred (27:52-53), and an "earthquake" (27:54) came as Jesus died on the cross. These barely supersede the phenomena said to have attended the death of Mary. But Christ was special: the God-man (John 1:1; I John 1:1-2) was dying for a special cause (John 12:27):

> *Well might the sun in darkness hide*
> *And shut his glories in*
> *When Christ the mighty maker died*
> *For man the creature's sin.*

Isaac Watts

Pope Pius XII enunciated the dogma of the Assumption in 1950 (p. 92). A crowd estimated at about nine hundred thousand became ecstatic at the pronouncement, in and near the basilica of St. Peter's.

The value of any statement of belief that received "official" notification "on earth" approximately thirteen to nineteen centuries after the fact makes one wonder. Have the intervening generations of believers been shortchanged? If not, what is its value?

Does Mary begin to rise here to the same level of the Christ? Was a cosmic escalator after all moving her upward from humanity to Deity, rewarding her for her days of virginity? Did papacy supply the final revolution of divine mechanics that produced a real queen in heaven to help sustain a not quite self-contained King? If so, are we back in Greek and Roman mythology?

Scripture later called Jesus King of Kings and Lord of Lords (Revelation 17:14). Scripture is fair and kind to Mary but she never receives a promotion from the status of a *bona fide* human being to a member of celestial royalty.

Looking to the ultimate Source Book of the Christian faith, we find that "the queen of heaven" (found only in Jeremiah 44:17-25) never refers to one of divine or godly status but to one of the stellar constellations (i.e., as an idol or object of worship forbidden to God's people but practiced in heathen countries).

Here the genius of the Christian revelation is at stake. We know an idea more accurately when we know it historically. The New Testament gives an historical account of the birth of Christianity, including Christ's life, death, resurrection, and His control of His church through the Spirit afterward. A sharp example of historical accuracy is whether Peter was the "rock" on which Christ built His church (see ch. six, B. Theology).

Neither Peter nor others thought Jesus meant special power only for him in Matthew 16:18, because in Matthew 18:1 they were arguing which was to be greatest. This same language He used for all disciples in John 20:23.

The importance of Jesus' authority appears on p. 51 in *Alone of All Her Sex*, in view of Matthew 19:13. Jesus, head of His church, spoke pungently, leaving celibacy to the choice of the individual kingdom servant: "For there are eunuchs who were born so from their mother's womb; and there are eunuchs, who were made so by men; and there are eunuchs, who have made themselves eunuchs for the kingdom of heaven. He that can take, let him take it." (Matthew 19:12, Douay Version). This paragraph does not record an isolated event. Those striving with celibacy deserve sympathy. A system of authoritarianism demanding it opposes Christ's teaching, Peter's practice (Mark 1:30,34), and Christian liberty (Matt. 19:13 and I Cor. 9:5). This incident,

36

together with Jesus' statement in Matthew 19:13 (Douay Version) clearly shows that marriage is optional for any representative of the church.

III. MARY AS BRIDE

Chapter eight, on The Song of Songs (pp. 121-133), depicts a spiral-shaped single valve of marine origin that portrays Christ and Mary seated beside each other on a throne. It is almost as a throne built for two. The Virgin has serious eyes and a countenance of determination. Her role in sharing a throne with Christ seems to fulfill beautifully the function of queen. Both Christ and Mary hover over the church in this projection, apparently, with the appearance of deity, magnifying or confirming Mary's role as queen.

Pope Innocent II (A.D. 1130-43), by virtue of his solemnizing this creation, is at the right side of Mary and immediately adjacent to a model of a Christian house of worship. Thus Pope and Madonna join Christ in hovering over the church. The description of such artistic creativity generates the desire to travel more and see firsthand what elaborate and moving concepts have resulted from combining art, religion, altruistic aesthetics, and the innate human yearning for power. Chapters nine through eleven, under Bride, are equally intriguing and for the same reasons.

Madonna (chapter ten, pp. 149-159) is usually "my lady," and long has referred to the Virgin Mary. Madonna has possibly come to be the most widely known term for Mary.

The material exudes the mystical influence of the Madonna, causing the poet ultimately to call upon both the name of God as well as holy Mary as though they were synonymous.

There is a kind of special guardianship over priests by Mary, and many of the narratives are typical of this era (possibly A.D. 1500 through 1700). She gave protection to their celibacy (p. 158). The narrative toward the bottom of page 158 laments with illustrations the excesses of its equivalent of the Counter Reformation. Emotion of the reaction to the Reformation was at its height.

Mary appears to be the patroness to love among couples in this life, being the ladylike epitome, and no other person was comparable to her. To think about Mary was supposed to be a priest's counterattack on evil thought. Helpful in numerous cases, it sometimes acted in reverse (pp. 158-159).

IV. Mary as Mother

The doctrine of the Immaculate Conception (ch. sixteen, pp. 236-254), as we have tried to understand it, is possibly one of the strongest evidences of a durable vein of commendable ascetism in all Roman Catholic teaching.

After stating that the New Testament presents no material to deny the presence of sin in the virgin, what we usually call "original" or "inherited," the church fathers nonetheless, although they exuded much praiseful language for Mary's supernatural power over evil as a virgin, did refuse to announce her as entirely immune from original sin or wholly released from the grip of inherited sin.

While the Immaculate Conception is one of the strongest doctrines of Catholicism, and while Marina Warner gives it one of the best treatments we have analyzed, the genius of Christianity is attenuated by the idea that Mary was characterized by permanent virginity. The supposition that she never had normal wifely relations with Joseph is illogical and irrelevant to Christ's mission, especially in the face of Matthew's words, "Then Joseph . . . took unto him his wife . . . "And he knew her not till she brought forth her firstborn son: and he called his name JESUS" (Matt. 1:25, Douay Version).

The doctrine of perpetual virginity for Mary is patently superfluous though not abstrusely so. It is not needed to grant Christ either soteriological powers or sinlessness.

The "tendency to sin" which we all have come to grips with both in reality as well as in theological studies, is not the same as original sin or any other kind of sin. Therefore when the author of Hebrews says that Christ "was in all points tempted like as we are, yet without sin" (Hebrews 4:15, Douay Version), it is real. Christ came to grips with the world, the flesh, and the devil.

The need for the doctrine had incited many to derive from the concept of Mary's nobility and glorious achievements more than is warranted either by history, the Bible, or from logic. The role of Jesus as our Saviour, as the one who bore our sins, as the one who was raised from the dead in order to demonstrate that He had plucked the chief fruit from sin which was and is death and that therefore He died a victorious death over sin, is all intact as much without the doctrine of the Immaculate Conception as with it.

Is this, therefore, a subconscious urge to ascribe to Mary goddesshood? Even in the Roman Empire later, the tendency was almost a way of life. The Roman wing of the Christian faith was victimized by it. It is not in Scripture. Spiritual awakenings have not come from it. It detracts from the distinctly Christian concept of the absolute lordship of Christ. This question is serious, is it then Christian?

Chapter thirteen (pp. 192-205) shows Mary as the ideal of motherhood in its totality. Even so, Mary as mother, by a unique dispensation of the sovereign God, is wholly free from the conjugal relation, from birth pangs, and from all phenomena associated with childbirth. The only function from the standpoint of biology that is conceded to her in the cult is the phenomenon of nursing a baby. From the very initial pictures of her, the female progenitress of Deity appears as attending to the hunger pangs of her baby (p. 192).

The subject of nursing associated with Mary may have begun in the northernmost country of Africa, namely the land of the Pharaohs. In Ur of the Chaldees, some two millenniums prior to the coming of Jesus, a goddess consented for her son to have access to her source of milk. Even in Mexico images have appeared that can possibly be dated back as far as one millennium prior to Christ. This is true to a lesser degree in other parts of Africa and even in India.

The milk of Mary, when related to her function in interceding and effecting therapy, generated numerous relics of various kinds in Europe. Containers supposedly conserving her milk were at a premium as objects of reverence and homage (p. 200). The efficacy of Mary's milk took it even to the burning lips in the place of purging where the dead had arrived (p. 200).

V. Intercessor

> *"Hail, Mary, full of grace, the Lord is with thee; blessed art thou amongst women, and blessed is the fruit of thy womb, Jesus. Holy Mary, Mother of God, pray for us sinners, now and at the hour of our death. Amen."*

The foregoing copy of the *Hail Mary* we memorized in youth. Often its lines have suggested how good it would be to have "somebody special" to escort us across the river of death. Or, if that is not admissible, to have a representative of Heaven, especially a member of the "family" of Heaven with us at death (see esp. John 14:3). We do have "somebody special," a word directly from headquarters answers! It is the Holy Spirit, God Himself, the Third Person of the Trinity, who comes into our hearts at the time we first believe on Christ and He remains there forever (John 3:8c, 15-16; Col. 1:27).

Mary, bless her for all she has done for us, cannot do that. To do so she would first have to be *omniscient* and be able to hear intelligently millions, thousands, or at least dozens of prayers at the same time. Second, she would have to be *omnipotent*. But cult and myth cannot raise a delightful personality from the human level to the divine. God the Father, God the Son, and God the Holy Spirit are co-equal, co-eternal, and co-existent. They had neither beginning nor end. So in "the hour of our death" we personally shall be trusting fully Jesus Christ, who shall be the first whose face we behold in eternity (Hebrews 12:1-2). He has already died for us. He has tasted death (Mark 9:1)! But now He lives.

Jesus, Saviour, pilot me
Over life's tempestuous sea;
Unknown waves before me roll,
Hiding rock and treach'rous shoal;
Chart and compass came from Thee:
Jesus, Saviour, pilot me.

Edward Hopper

Almighty God gave Mary two assignments, which precluded any further responsibility for her in Christ's mission. They were (1) to be his human mother and (2) to supply the home that the Messiah of Hebrew origin needed for early training.

The Savior must be divine and human. His mother, therefore, must be fully human. To be less, she could not properly supply his humanity; to be more than human, she would only be duplicating the work of the Holy Spirit.

Mary does not have any assignment in the intercessory work of Christ: "For there is one God, and one mediator between God and men, the man Christ Jesus;" (1 Tim. 2:5). Scripture limits the Intercessor in two ways. First, He is thoroughly "man." Second, the intercession is limited to "one," because the atoning death could come through only one. To have more than one (beyond Christ) or to have someone who is not "man" would disqualify him. With atoning death, Christ alone was qualified to intercede (Isaiah 53:12 and Hebrews 7:25).

Notes

1. A. T. Robertson, *An Introduction to the Textual Criticism of the New Testament,* Sunday School Board of the S.B.C., Nashville, Tennessee, 1925, p. 22.

2. A. Merriam-Webster, *Webster's New Collegiate Dictionary,* G & C Merriam Publishers, Springfield, Mass. 1961, p. 202.

3. Marina Warner, *Alone of All Her Sex,* Alfred A. Knopf, New York. 1976.

4. Ibid., XIX-XXV.

5. John Ferguson, *Religions of the Roman Empire,* Cornell University Press, Ithaca, New York, 1974, p. 29.

6. Ibid., p. 30f.

4

"Whatsoever He Shall Say to You, Do Ye" (Mary to the Servants, in John 2:5, Douay-Rheims)

Only two conversations between Mary and Jesus appear in the Bible. The first occurred in Jerusalem at the Temple when Jesus was twelve years old (Luke 2:41-51). The second was at a marriage in Cana of Galilee (John 2:1-11). This occurred in the midst of domestic issues that this mother extraordinary had faced with her unique son daily for about thirty years. A home issue would be the area of expertise for humanity's most famous mother.

The most gala occasion in Galilee is a wedding. The bride is the center of attention as never before or after. The groom is king for almost a week.

The night before the wedding, festive affairs accompanied by bonfires prevail until early dawn. Women chant slogans by the hour such as "*Arusetna imneecha*" ("Our bride is nice, wonderful"). The whole community becomes aware of the impending event.

Mary was present at "a marriage in Cana of Galilee" (John 2:1, Douay Version). Being a capable, gregarious woman, she was highly respected long before the cause of her ultimate fame had spread through the world. She may have attended the wedding as a relative of the bride.

Jesus and his closer friends were present: "And Jesus also was invited (*eklēthē*) and his disciples to the marriage" (John

2:2, Douay Version). Jesus' humanity and sociability were evident from the beginning. He was Man. He could thirst, be hungry, get tired (John 4:6-8), and enjoy the fellowship of jubilant friends. Neither Jesus nor the disciples were social misfits or eccentric men.

WHEN MARY ADVISED JESUS

Suddenly, a disturbing note intruded: "They have no wine," Mary said (John 2:3b, Douay Version). For so meaningful an occasion, this was a radical disruption of custom.

Jesus' response to Mary appears brusque: "Woman, what is that to me and to thee? My hour is not yet come" (John 2:4, Douay Version).

"Woman" is formal. Jesus used it from the cross, "Woman, behold thy son," committing the earthly care of Mary to John—spontaneous love for her who gave Him birth (John 19:26). As the oldest son, Jesus assumed responsibility for Mary according to Jewish primogeniture. Jesus' compassion and humanity were evident from the beginning, as was His sociability.

This formal term *Woman* kept Mary in fair juxtaposition with her son. Zeal for the unbiblical phrase "mother of God" would come soon enough. Those who assumed that the purpose of the Virgin Birth was to get a queen in heaven for the "divine family" instead of a savior on earth for the human family later coined the phrase. "The Council of Chalcedon (A.D. 451) perhaps the most important of all councils since Nicaea . . . condemned Nestorius . . . because Nestorius refused to call Mary 'the mother of God.' "[1]

Mary only made a suggestion to Jesus at the wedding. It was not even a request, much less a supplication or prayer. It was barely a hint. "They have no wine" (John 2:3, Douay Version).

It does not savor of matriarchal hauteur or of talking down to Deity. She was Jesus' earthly mother. Such down-to-earth household exchanges likely had been frequent in everyday life. She would have to get used to doing without them (Mark 3:33-34, 6:3-5).

Mary's hint, "They have no wine," did not leave the impression that her role as human mother gave her control over kingdom principles, much less over the King himself. Reducing the time nature required to make wine from months to a few seconds, Jesus showed Deity to be in control of the laws He had made (John 1:3). The honor of being the human channel through which He entered the human race was Mary's unique reward.

WHEN MARY ADVISED OTHERS

Mary "saith to the waiters" bearing the water pots, "Whatsoever he shall say to you, do ye" (John 2:5, Douay Version). These words came from the warm concern of a mother's heart.

The mission of her son she would sympathetically understand. Her motive in stating this request may have been to get one of the most realistic, dynamic principles of victorious living before the company and ultimately before all the world: "Whatsoever he shall say to you, do ye." The principle of obedience to lofty principle is as applicable in the home as it is anywhere.

Mary advised others only this once, as far as the records show. But this was enough because of (1) its clarity, and (2) its inclusiveness. "Whatsoever" shows her confidence in the absolute wisdom and power of Christ. These Mary did not claim for herself. Obedience to Christ proved successful in confronting this domestic problem. Jesus proceeded to turn several pots of water into about forty-two and one-half gallons of table wine.

Jesus added, "My hour is not yet come" (John 2:4) because turning water into wine was His first miracle and came early in His ministry. The plan of redemption called for His dying at a certain time and place. It must come after adequate time for training the disciples against the day when He would no longer be with them. He would gear all His ministry to this schedule. He repeated this idea often in the gospels. Mary equipped Christ with humanity for His role to bring atonement and for Him to become our intercessor as Isaiah predicted (Isa. 53:12). According to the Bible, God did not complicate her role by adding to it functions in atonement and intercession.

She could rest securely having done her assignment well to the end. To extend her function beyond supplying Christ's human nature to match the divine would detract from His unique Lordship and appear to fragment the impenetrable Trinity concept so closely guarded in the baptismal formula (Matt. 28:19-20) and the apostolic benediction (II Cor. 13:14).

By "my hour is not yet come," Jesus clearly told Mary that (1) He alone could accomplish His work of redemption and intercession, and that (2) the literal timing of His work in atonement (crucifixion) only the cosmic calendar would determine. He would instruct those whom He healed not to tell what they knew about Him because His hour had not come (See esp. Mark 5:4-3; John 12:23-27).

The tension and formal break with the Jewish ecclesiastics would come soon enough, with His crucifixion following immediately. The way He synchronized everything else with it is amazing. Mary believed Jesus' word on any subject to be accurate and that all believers could act on it in confidence.

The trouble with the world today is that men are not heeding the Blessed Virgin. What did she say do? She said do what Jesus said to do: "Whatsoever he shall say to you, do ye." Many are stumbling over the simplicity of these words into misery, mistakes, and the mirage of distorted spiritual concepts.

REJECTING MARY'S ADVICE

The pope twice in 1493 strictly ordered all except the Spanish and Portuguese that America (or the Western Hemisphere) was not for them.

"At the insistence of Ferdinand and Isabella, Pope Alexander VI issued two bulls, *Inter Caetera I* and *II,* which granted to Spain all lands not under Christian rule and set a line at one hundred leagues (263 miles) west of the Azores and Cape Verde

Islands, beyond which all future discoveries not held by a Christian ruler on 25 December 1492 would belong to Spain. This was in May 1493."[2] Christian ruler here means Roman Catholic.

"Bull" is from Latin *bulla*, which Webster defines as "a papal letter sealed with a bulla, or with a red-ink imprint of the device on the bulla, because of the significance of its subject matter . . . an imperial edict, as of the Holy Roman Empire."[3] The equating of a "papal letter" (pronouncement of the pope) to "an imperial edict" of a nation is recognition that the Vatican with its political hierarchical organization headed by a monarch is a state, a government, much like the United States or France except that it has a sprawling religious appendage called the Vatican (originally the hill around St. Peter's chapel). Vaticanism means absolute papal supremacy, according to Webster.

Jesus, whom Mary told others to obey (John 3:2), said "Love your enemies" (Matt. 5:44, Douay Version). He did not say to order them around in *bullas* or burn them at the stake.

Burnings at the stake were common prior to and during the Reformation. But among the forces struggling in the never-ending cosmic dialectic are some political entities that adopt any front to dominate or at least to remain viable. Some are always striving to rule, reign, or control dictatorially. Historical facts are indispensable for a fair approach. The ancient Roman Empire did not die. Weakened, it assumed a new form.

American schools used to expose students to the Reformation and its gory details, as well as to its most sacred principles, which are basic to democratic life. We memorized in public high school dates like July 6, 1415, when John Huss was burned at the stake. Such men usually assumed the authority of Scripture over the authority of the papacy. About the time of John Huss's death, the holdings of the clergy of the church (priests and mostly bishops) amounted to about 50 percent of all the land of Bohemia.[4] John Huss was accused of heresy because he did not agree with the established church.

Hugh Latimer (b. 1485 in Leicestershire—d. Oct. 16, 1555 at Oxford) was a Protestant of English heritage who championed the Reformation through his extraordinary preaching. He derived his doctrinal position from Scripture. He was arraigned, arrested, and removed to Oxford to be tried. There he was burned at the stake together with Nicholas Ridley on October 16, 1555. History has immortalized Latimer for his cry just before burning to death at the hands of the state church. Addressing his comrade in martyrdom, he said, "Be of good comfort Master Ridley, and play the man; . . . we shall this day light such a candle, by God's grace, in England as I trust shall never be put out."[5] The fire of the bodies of Ridley and Latimer has not gone out—yet.

American constitutionalism has held consistently that a parent is not discriminated against by not being able to send his child to a "religious" school supported by the government. This is the way the founding fathers created the constitution. People who do not like secular schools supported by the state knew about them before they came. Some have developed antipathy for them by being involved with ecclesiastical patterns that get state support for their schools in Europe.

If Ridley and Latimer's light should subside temporarily, it will burn brightly again. Even though Roman Catholicism owns about three-fourths of all parochial schools in America, what it teaches cannot defeat biblical revelation.

Secular humanists who resent seeing a vigorous part-state, part-church striving to get an iron grip upon this comparatively new nation by domineering the school enterprise, have their own liberty endangered.

The state rigidly requires education. If the school requires and teaches religion and the state supports the school, then the state is teaching religion. The framers of the Constitution had learned from their experience and wrote accordingly, "Congress shall make no law respecting an establishment of religion . . ." A law permitting income tax deductions for tuition paid to parochial schools would set the nation back over 200 years. A law respecting religion is not necessarily religion respecting law.

Some historical volumes record the prominent and strategic burnings, as though they were rare. But some proceed to show the politico-religious fanaticism that permeated life when this part-state, part-religion was about to lose its absolutistic dicta-

48

torial hold on the people. For example, Reformer John Wycliffe, (1330-1384) missed stake-burning, so they exhumed his remains, burned them, and reputedly scattered them on the Thames River.[6]

Devotees of horror movies can improve their fare by reading accounts of the burning of women by state-church authorities. In *Foxe's Book of Martyrs*, edited by G. A. Williamson, are the accounts of numerous persons who were tortured and burned at the stake for holding onto their faith.[7]

If indeed the Creator of man and the universe, Christ in John 1:3, favored the existence of a nation with freedom, like the Edenic principle in the Garden, and biblicism in its background like that of the United States, then the opposition of Romanism to the U.S. Constitution and life are in defiance of Mary, who urged men to do as Christ wants them to do. Such defiance generated untold suffering for the early settlers of America. It complicated life miserably for them, socially and religiously, about the time the dark clouds of the thousand years of darkness were beginning to rise.

In September 1493 Columbus set sail a second time, not with three ships and ninety reluctant men, but with an imposing armada of seventeen ships bearing over twelve hundred men (no women), at least five priests, livestock, seeds, and building materials, showing that Spain had made a serious colonizing effort that would be followed by countless others before the revolutions of the nineteenth century collapsed her American Empire.[8]

You can better understand Pope Alexander VI issuing such bulls or edicts to control the Western Hemisphere and other major segments of the world by recalling his background. Teachers and predecessors had long indoctrinated him with the concept of unlimited papal authority and "infallibility," possibly since early impressionable childhood. Otherwise, this action by a religious leader or head of a church is practically unbelievable to contemporary Americans. From any standpoint it is the opposite of American ideology, liberty, national life, and constitutionalism. This head of a church had accepted the Roman but non-Christian idea that his church was also a state. He had in effect a thorough parochial school background. For the United States to grant income tax deductions for tuition paid to parochial schools may be underwriting the ideology and methodology of Pope Alexander VI, who tried to limit the Western Hemisphere to two wholly Roman Catholic countries!

Adherents are historically correct in holding to the name Roman Catholic. All popes for 400 years have been Roman, save one or perhaps two. It strives to be universal, or *catholic*, as the *bullas* showed.

Holding such historical facts in purview can help United States officials and citizens make decisions in the capitol or at the polls.

The discovery and development of America coincided with the Protestant Reformation. While the Reformation began in A.D. 1517 with Luther's *Ninety-five Theses* on the church door in Wittenburg, Germany, the Reformation largely determined the kind of people who settled America from 1492 to 1812. Only thus could America have given liberty to both Protestants and Catholics. Until after 1812, Protestants comprised at least 95 percent of the population. By 1776 the total population was near 3.5 million.

Puritan Christians, from one-fourth to one-half of the colonial population at times, were strict in self-discipline. However, they learned to live amicably with Christians of many kinds, including those that were not so strict. (See esp. *Puritan Age in Massachusetts*, by George E. Ellis; pub. by Burt Franklin, New York.)

In view of the incomparable purity of Mary as well as her loyalty to her son's teachings (Acts 1:14), her sympathy for those who would be seeking to establish puritanism would be natural. "John Hooper, Bishop of Gloucester during these years, has been justifiably named the 'father' of Puritanism."[9] John Calvin became its foremost interpreter and staunchest promoter. To answer the question, "What Frenchman more than any other caused more Americans to be monogamists, Puritans, respecters of temperance, practitioners of personal honesty and integrity?" requires two words: John Calvin. The "church-state" of Europe had persecuted the settlers of the original thirteen colonies out of Europe, with few exceptions.

"There were more than three million people in the original thirteen colonies in 1776 and only twenty-two thousand were non-Protestant Christians."[10] *The Democratic Experience* states that the population of the United States in 1800 was 5,308,433.[11]

Though a "state" church was and is less productive of biblical faith and of vigorous ethical and moral life, it was the only kind the early settlers had known in Catholic Europe where state-churchism forbade them access to the Bible.

Puritanism's ideal of renewed personal integrity, with the church ever striving toward biblical standards and patterns, may seem irrelevant in this day of promiscuity, laissez faire morals, bribery, dishonesty, addiction, and intemperance. But the only alternative to puritanism is "impuritanism." This includes hate leading to murder and robbery, broken homes, more children of the latter and the concomitant burden to the public, slavery to carnal impulses and a decrease in respect for the character qualities conducive to producing altruistic citizens.

Having tried the state-church concept, as nine of the thirteen colonies did,[12] they had learned experientially whether they wanted it or not. When the Constitution was framed and began operating in 1789 under the leadership of George Washington, no established church appeared under state or federal auspices. By experimentation the colonists knew it as a failure, that it leads to unfair favoritism, and carries a built-in seed box of ill will. Therefore the United States, possibly the greatest government of all time, has had no state church, and thus far its Supreme Court has ruled without exception against even token financial favoritism. That the court will so rule again is the firm conviction of many.

The Edenic principle reappeared in the United States, without any modification or qualifications, beginning in 1789. Each man thus has the right to live as he thinks best, according to the light given him with one limitation: his liberty ends where his neighbor's begins. Otherwise, he is as free to do wrong as he is to do right, to belong to a church or not.

Religious liberty in the United States is more than the right to belong to the church of one's choice. It is more than the privilege of going to or supporting a church without being persecuted. It assures that no other church or religion may have an unfair built-in advantage of government support for church schools or the prestigious advantage of a foreign "state" status like the Vatican and its dubious status as "successor" of the Holy Roman Empire. Only the U.S.A. has this liberty!

A parent cherishes his child's affection when freely bestowed. A normal father or mother does not want his child to love him if he has to force or bribe him to secure an expression of affection. God Almighty wanted Adam and his descendants volitionally to believe in and love Him. If they had had no choice in the matter, God is not honored by it. Voluntarism is basic to all Christian action, including right living and support of one's church (Acts 5-6; Philemon 14).

The nine original colonies that did have state churches for a while simply knew no better. They were from Europe where they had never seen anything except a monolithic ecclesiastical structure. When they had freedom in Colonial America, the religious group in the majority exercised authority, became "established," and sometimes did what they had seen in the old world; namely, they punished, fined, discriminated against, and persecuted dissenters. The nine colonies were Massachusetts, Connecticut, New Hampshire, all of which wanted the Puritan Congregational church; Virginia, New York, Maryland, North Carolina, South Carolina, and Georgia were all strongly committed to the Anglican (contemporary Episcopalian) ecclesiastical pattern.

Rhode Island was the only colony that originated in America and not on the continent (Europe). It alone vouchsafed genuine religious liberty for all dwellers. (See the volume *Church and State in the United States*, by Anson Phelps Stokes and Leo Pfeffer, Harper and Brothers, New York, 1950, for one of the finest treatments of religion vis-à-vis the government in the colonies. Stokes shows the attitude and practice in each case and gives an accurate picture, apparently, of each colony—especially pp. 3-13.)

Having seen what the settling of the escapees from religious persecution in Europe has brought to the world, it is difficult to imagine the Virgin Mary, if she can see things here, not smiling with maternal satisfaction upon the many accomplishments that

52

have occurred in a nation founded largely by men who sought to obey Mary's son as she requested in John 2:5. While this nation is imperfect, it has set the stage, given man personal liberty, and kept the doors open to democratic life for all, for freely interpreting and practicing the teachings of Christ.

The future is brighter for Catholics, Protestants, and secularists because of American liberty. The Bible has been the chief Source Book of her religion. The law forbidding any church or religion to have a governmentally structured advantage over others was not primarily the result of everybody being so good and altruistic. Rather it was the fear of the aggressiveness of some and the ever-present possibility of unfair tactics by others.

Surely Mary would have found it difficult to smile on the two papal bulls in 1493 (*Inter Caetera Roman I and II*) that "granted to Spain all lands not under Christian rule."[13] The second bull decreed that "all lands discovered not held by a Christian ruler on 25 December 1492 would belong to Spain." This was in May 1493.[14] Would Mary have smiled upon the kind of society that they would have brought to the Western world? Instead of our liberty, we would have had state churches, possibly burnings at the stake like Europe was having at the time, and a scarcity of Bibles instead of the freedom that finally prevailed, providentially.

Spain made an enthusiastic effort to colonize in the West, as did other nations of Europe. But the pressure and counterpressures of the old continent would bring on revolutions and the war of the nineteenth century that would nullify the outreach of Spain in the West in general and in America in particular.[15]

The welding together spiritually of the thirteen original colonies is unique history. The United States of America is so unique a nation that its addition of other states continues even down to the present and could possibly attest the probability of its divinely ordained origin.

That the source of authority in religion is the Bible has been the posture historically in Protestant Christendom. Christ said, ". . . and the scripture cannot be broken" (John 10:35, Douay Version). *Cannot be broken* means *inter alia,* "to annul, subvert; to do away with, to deprive of authority, whether by precept or act."[16] Thus the Founder of the Christian faith said that the source of authority for religious reality is Scripture, often called "the Word of God." *A Hand Book of the Catholic Faith* also calls the Bible the Word of God and classifies this as the highest compliment for a book.[17] Note that the title carries *Catholic* to identify it, not *Christian.*

Depending upon Scripture for the content of the faith voids subjectivism, whether papal, priestly, or that proceeding from the laity. Dozens of authors spread through more than fourteen hundred years write unitedly on one theme, in the Bible.

Those of us who respect Peter as an apostle find a most rewarding surprise when we start taking him seriously. To esteem him as first of the apostles in any sense and then ignore his express teachings is inconsistent. This apostle many hold to be their first pope. Peter says to them, "And account the longsuffering of our Lord, salvation; as also our most dear brother Paul, according to the wisdom given him, hath written you: As also in all his epistles, speaking in them of these things; in which are certain things hard to be understood, which the unlearned and unstable wrest, as they do also the other scriptures, to their own destruction" (2 Peter 3:15-16, Douay Version).

Peter commanded here that we give heed to "all his [Paul's] epistles" (2 Peter 3:16). Peter said "all" and not to just one or two of Paul's epistles or statements. Not to obey the erudite Paul by heeding all his epistles has already resulted in the "destruction" of many, said Peter. The King James Version translates in effect in the same way. Those who "wrest" this scripture out of its context, that is, give Paul's writings in the Bible a meaning and application that they do not have and which Paul did not intend them to have; such people bring upon themselves "destruction" (2 Peter 3:16).

Paul, whom Peter commanded us to obey and revere to save us from "destruction," wrote, that "In us you may learn, that one be not puffed up against the other for another, above that which is written" (I Cor. 4:6, Douay Version).

Practically all the griefs, errors, heresies, and radicalism that have come into church life have been the result of going above or beyond that which is written. To avoid going "above [beyond] that which is written" is Paul's specific command here. And Peter has commanded that Paul should not be ignored. Going "above [beyond] that which is written" needs to be pondered by those who want Christianity, the revelation of God in Christ, not the myth, cult, lore, and tradition which make void the word of God. Even Mark warned stringently against "making void the word of God by your own tradition, which you have given forth" (Mark 7:13). How many life-giving aspects of Christianity are left undone merely because we are following some man-made tradition instead of following the word of God?

If we accept Peter's authority at all, we should be consistent and do what he teaches. Peter commanded that we heed *all* Paul had written. Paul commanded believers not to go "above that which is written." The *New American Bible* translates this, "May you learn from us not to go beyond what is set down . . ." (I Cor. 4:6). Referring imperatively to the divinely ordained source of religious authority, we are not to go beyond Scripture, the one and only Bible given by the Lord to guide and teach sinners. What we believe about Christ and His entire family, including Mary, we should receive from Scripture only—not myth, tradition, cult, lore and custom.

Jesus also said that Scripture is Christ-evidencing. The Bible is the written Word; Christ is the living Word. The Bible's great value is that it reveals Christ accurately in the leadership of God's Spirit. "Search the scriptures, for you think in them to have life everlasting; and the same are that give testimony of me" (John 5:39, Douay Version). The immediate purpose of Christianity appears in John 17:39. "Now this is eternal life: That they may know thee, the only true God, and Jesus Christ, whom thou hast sent" (John 17:3, Douay Version).

The word *new* about some element of an old product usually gives it another lease on life and a boost in sales. The mania for something "new" in religion never subsides. Paul predicted, "For there shall be a time, when they shall not endure sound doctrine; but, according to their own desires, they will heap up to themselves teachers, having itching ears: and will indeed turn away their hearing from the truth, but will be turned unto fables" (II

Tim. 4:3-4, Douay Version). For this reason America, with its forward-looking, investigative, exploratory, even scientific and philosophical inclination, has produced a number of "new" religions and some new twists to the old. We do not question the right or freedom of anyone to do so, so long as the religion does not hurt others. But examples of the hurtful are not lacking.

On November 18, 1978, over 900 California people under the religious leadership of Reverend (?) Jim Jones went to their death by a mass suicide pact in Guyana, South America. The total number has been estimated from 912 to 920 for this religious mass suicide covenant.

Scientology was reviewed in *Reader's Digest*, May 1980, under the title, "Anatomy of a Frightening Cult" (pp. 86ff). The *Digest* writers made a modest estimate of Scientology's worldwide annual income of millions of dollars. Scientology has a strong defense under the title, *The Truth About Scientology,* copyrighted by Trevor Meldal-Johnson and Joseph Rusey. References to "brushes" with the FBI, the USAF (p. 4f), the IRS (p. 5), and CIA (p. 5), the AMA (p. 5), the Labor Department (p. 5), and others, appear to some degree therein. Every American is free to read and make up his own mind. This too is freedom, freedom to read, study, use the mind to draw conclusions (Mark 1:4, 15).

Meanwhile, a look at the religion of the Founding Fathers could be illimitably profitable. Its Founder predicted the increasing deceit of false religions (Matt. 24:11-12) The stability of His followers strengthens a nation: "By this shall all men know that you are my disciples, if you have love one for another" (John 13:35, Douay Version). This is the kind of love wherein the lover is more concerned for the well-being of the object of his affection than he is for his own welfare.

This is superior to assuming a posture of being "persecuted" or "discriminated against" if your religion does not receive a preferential status above others. It elicits respect.

The tax-free operation of mosques in the United States merits respectful attention. Present laws on religious freedom are not being violated. Newly arrived religions are doing what *some* of "the old" have been trying to do all along, namely take advantage of a tax-free status vis-à-vis the government.

The innate sympathy and unstudied respect of most Americans for anything called "religious" leaves some like babes in the woods. The theology of the Moslem faith has available sources. Better still, one can read the Koran. (See *Koran, Secret Writings —The Harvard Classics*, trans. by E. H. Palmer, esp. "The Chapter of Women," p. 973). Apparently their theologians assume sex life continues in the next world.

The Koran does not give the definition of "holy war," with its implications for soldiers who get killed in and for those who survive a battle, according to Islamic tradition. But every American ought to know what Moslems teach and believe about it. The Founder of Christianity said in Mark 12:24, "And Jesus answering, saith to them: do ye not therefore err, because you know not the scriptures, nor the power of God?" (Douay Version). The Lord then reaffirmed that the source of religious authority is the Bible or the word of God. Then he added, "For when they shall rise again from the dead, they shall neither marry, nor be married, but are as the angels in heaven" (Mark 12:24-25, Douay Version). Thus gender as a functional distinction ceases with resurrection and the fully arrived kingdom of God.

Has the time come for a reconsideration of all tax-free privileges for any religion including Christianity? It would cost many old-line churches dearly. But it could cost the nation more in ultimate effect on a constituency partly naive and partly wily. The generosity of the United States government to religion evolved in an era when the prevalent Puritanism ideology centered on producing good people.

American generosity to religions evolved, or came at times spontaneously, in the wake of colonial days of early nationhood, when half the people were striving toward Puritanism. The churches produced good, moral, hardworking citizens. Today increasing numbers are aspiring and striving to rule, to bleed the government financially, or to hitch a ride to their own material advantage. Spiritual values and good citizenship are far down the list of priorities if they are on the list at all. Is the time propitious for taxing religion? Is at least a reconsideration of the favored status of "religion" and churches urgent? Where religion has become an economic enterprise, the "religious" would not suffer.

Where spiritual values are still paramount, believers could endure it.

An occasional aberration, expression of extremism, or witch hunt almost inevitably appears where deeply committed people are dealing with what they hold to be the most pertinent factors of time and eternity. This is all the more reason why a democratic government like the U.S.A. should be on hand always to keep the stage props arranged democratically. "Power corrupts. Absolute power corrupts absolutely." This is not as simple as administering antitrust laws and pure food requirements. It is just as necessary.

The trouble with the world today, as well as before 1492, is that men do not heed the Blessed Virgin. What did she say do? She said do what Jesus said do: "Whatsoever he shall say to you, do ye" (John 2:5).

Many early American settlers were fugitives from religious hierarchies and their resulting restrictive living. The Constitution today permits each to choose his religious affiliation or lack of affiliation. IT ALSO PREVENTS ONE RELIGION FROM SECURING A POLITICAL ADVANTAGE OVER OTHERS. NINE OF THE ORIGINAL THIRTEEN COLONIES HAD STATE CHURCHES. Framers of the Constitution did not like that (see footnote 10 by J. M. Dawson, p. 58 herein).

Religion with hierarchical control has never produced a democratic country like the United States. Men debating over the Bible did. United States religious pluralism, its Constitution, and its goodwill have inspired numerous nations to seek this governmental pattern. Neither the widespread Moslem world nor the religious hierarchies of Europe have generated a country of *e pluribus unum* like the United States. Does the Constitution need a change now? America does not need either the national totalitarianism of the East or West, or religious authoritarianism from any other quarter. THE ONLY INCIPIENT VACUUM HERE IS THE LACK OF DEDICATION TO THE MORAL AND SPIRITUAL IDEALS OF THE BELIEVING MEN WHO CONCEIVED THIS NATION. Hierarchies have driven men to extreme socialism. Schools under such religions would be a step back toward what many early Americans had escaped.

Notes

1. *Illustrator*—Summer 1979, Materials Services Department, BSSB, 127 Ninth Avenue North, Nashville, Tennessee 37234 p. 36.

2. Sydney E. Ahlstrom, *A Religious History of the American People,* Yale University Press, New Haven, 1972, p. 37.

3. *Webster's New Collegiate Dictionary,* A Merriam-Webster, G & C. Merriam Co., Publishers, Springfield, Mass., U.S.A., copyright 1961, p. 110.

4. *Encyclopaedia Britannica,* Vol. II, William Benton, Publisher, Chicago, Ill. p. 910f.

5. Ibid., Vol. 13, p. 743.

6. Ibid., Vol. 23, p. 831.

7. G. A. Williamson, Editor, *Foxe's Book of Martyrs,* Little Brown and Company, Boston, 1965, pp. 328ff.

8. Sydney E. Ahlstrom, *A Religious History of the American People,* Yale University Press, New Haven, 1972, p. 37.

9. Clarence Ver Steeg, *The Formative Years, 1607-1763,* Hill and Wang, New York, 1968, p. 6.

10. J. M. Dawson, *Baptists and the American Republic,* Broadman Press, Nashville, Tennessee, 1956, p. 7.

11. *Democratic Experience,* Third Edition, Degler, Cochran, De Santis, Hamilton, Harbaugh, Link, Nye, Patter, Ver Steeg, Scott, Foresman and Company, Glenview, Illinois, 1973, p. 608.

12. J. M. Dawson, *Baptists and the American Republic,* Broadman Press, Nashville, Tennessee, 1956, p. 3.

13. Sydney E. Ahlstrom, *A Religious History of the American People,* Yale University Press, New Haven, 1972, p. 37.

14. Loc. cit.

15. Ibid., p. 37.

16. Joseph Henry Thayer, *Greek English Lexicon of the New Testament,* New York, Harper & Brothers, 1893, p. 385.

17. Dr. N.G.M. Van Doornck, *A Hand Book of the Catholic Faith,* Image Books, Doubleday and Company, Inc., Garden City, New York, 1956, p. 139.

5

"And You Shall Know the Truth, and the Truth Shall Make You Free" (Christ, in John 8:32, Douay-Rheims)

INTRODUCTION

These sketches of the colonies show the original religious inclination and background of early American settlers. Why settlers came over in the first place puts their heroism in the logic of history and compulsion of faith. Basic Americanism and the nature of the Constitution lie here.

The Thirteen Colonies and Their Dates

Virginia	1607	Delaware	1638
Massachusetts	1620	Pennsylvania	1643
New Hampshire	1622	North Carolina	1653
New York	1624	New Jersey	1660
Maryland	1634	South Carolina	1670
Connecticut	1635	Georgia	1733
Rhode Island	1636		

VIRGINIA (1607)

On May 2, 1607, three sailing ships arrived at the mouth of the James River with 105 English colonists. London and Plymouth entrepreneurs had sent them to settle in the Virginia area and they began "the history of the continuous Anglo American settlement."[1] (Dates of founding and chartering sometimes seem to differ.)

After failures fraught with suffering, sacrifice, and heroism, plus spending over 200,000 English pounds by the Virginia Company, they arrived. Of the 1,600 colonists sent by 1616 only 350 lived. The Jamestown settlement all but expired. "But Virginia survived, and the colony's unbroken church history begins immediately after the first landing."[2] They were Protestant, mostly Anglican.

John White (reaching Roanoke July, 1587) had found the earlier (1585-86) colonists at the mouth of the James River, not upstream as Raleigh instructed. Incapable of controlling people just released from life-long servility, he planned after a month's stay to return to England "for supplies."[3]

Britain was preparing for the Spanish Armada attack. So John White did not return to Roanoke Island, Virginia, until 1591. He had left, as evidence of his return, "his daughter and his granddaughter, Virginia Dare, the first English child born in America."[4]

England was in America to stay. America's language would be English; her legal, governmental, and cultural roots would be English, not of rich ancient Latin background. England, building a strong empire, becoming a naval power, and being a people of rich Protestant heritage and Bible religion, determined America's direction. The only alternative was the religion of Rome, half church and half state. Her Bible terms, names, ideas, and phrases were historically Christian, but Rome early restructured biblical terms and church life (c. A.D. 314) with the organization of the Roman Empire and its pantheon of heterogeneous religions. Christian terms and symbols became an appendage to the pantheon.

Christianity claims to be a revelation, not a religion. Man's descriptions of his striving toward God comprise religions. Christ's coming is a revelation (John 14:9; Philippians 2:5-11). Emperor Constantine's title became Pontifex Maximus. This is the pope's title today.

The early settlers were devout, and many were Anglicans (Episcopalians). The first representative assembly "met in the church at Jamestown in the summer of 1619, and was the first representative law-making body in English America and as such was the forerunner of representative government in the United States."[5] Protestant Britain began this.

The strength of the Church of England was such that they "held (1702) separate worship" even in so-called Catholic Maryland . . . ," and the Lord Baltimore would not allow the Jesuits in the colony to place any restrictions upon Protestants. (See chapter six under "Confusing Caesar's with God's.")

The prominence and dimensions of the Anglican Church in the early colonies by the late seventeenth century show in the figures of the Society for the Propagation of the Gospel that met in 1701—there were twenty thousand Anglicans living in Virginia and twenty thousand more in Maryland, and at least one thousand in New York. The number of clergymen in 1701 was estimated at fifty, with twenty-five of them in Virginia, seventeen in Maryland, and an average of one or more in the other colonies mentioned.

MASSACHUSETTS (1620)

This larger project of the Puritans included Plymouth of fame and sentiment. The Pilgrims dissolved the settlement and left as a final legacy to posterity the remarkable account of the "Plymouth Plantation," written by "their governor, the wise and virtuous William Bradford."[1]

These Puritans, possibly near midstream of rapidly changing English life at the time, held the Protestant Reformation to be unfinished (which it still is). They had long striven to "purify"[2] the Church of England. They wanted to eliminate "Romish" ceremonial traditions; to enforce Sabbath observances; to secure a better educated clergy; and to end the appointment of one clergyman to two or more income-yielding parishes. They wished to eliminate the absenteeism of priests who lived outside the parish. Augmenting the authority of local churches by reducing the authority of bishops was another goal.

The Calvinist background of James I gave them high hopes when he became king. But at the Hampton Court Conference in 1604 (more famous for inaugurating what became known as the King James Version of the Bible), James I disappointed them. He backed the bishops fully and told the Puritans he would "make them conform" or "harry them out of the land."[3] He first tried the latter. Then, soft or indifferent, James I did not do either. Charles I and Archbishop Laud, particularly between 1629 and 1640 when the Parliament did not convene, induced thousands to migrate to America. Most of them went to the burgeoning and prospering West Indies, but so many elected Massachusetts that it not only prospered rapidly but later spawned three additional colonies in the area.

In the early seventeenth century many in England were at variance with the Anglican state church. They regarded many clergymen as corrupt, irreligious, and they resented affluent, unspiritual clergymen who had little relationship with the common people and who put too much emphasis on ceremonialism. These dissenters were called Puritans. They felt worship should be simple and direct and dependent on the Bible. No one religious body has a monopoly on this responsibility or the means for achieving it. The Word and the Spirit are available to all.

Actually they did not wish to abandon the Anglican church; they aspired to "purify" it toward a greater commitment to the Christ of biblical revelation. Those who were fully "separatist" severed ties with the Anglican church. Government and state church made life so difficult for them that they moved to Holland. Deciding to start over in North America, their children would not be wholly like the Dutch ethnically.

In December 1620 the *Mayflower* and its "Pilgrims" made it to Plymouth. They called the place "Plymouth Colony," and in 1692 they gave it the status of a portion of Massachusetts. America has taken to its heart these Pilgrims, symbolically depicting the suffering they left behind and the courage in which they launched into a new life.

England was making the Puritans more miserable back home. To reform the Anglican Church was a hopeless task, they concluded. They would set up a true church shorn of hierarchical authoritarianism and ceremonialism. Actually they hoped to begin a democratic Puritan state for the people.[4]

In 1692 King Charles I gave the Puritans a land grant and charter called the Massachusetts Bay Company. The charter did not cover the subject of headquarters. Therefore the Puritans held their charter close to themselves and rejected locating its headquarters in England itself.

They wanted to have a "Bible Colony,"[5] and this was their opportunity. In March 1630 a small number of ships sailed from England with about 900 Puritan immigrants. They brought their charter, which mostly authorized them for trade and commerce. This was a serious advantage because it gave them the right to establish a government without interference from England. They highly regarded this charter as "their most precious possession, a symbol of their freedom, and as time went on they fought hard to keep it."[6]

Thus their faith led them through many hardships. "The ship's quartermaster gave each passenger a daily ration of food, and their passengers did their own cooking. The supplies included salt beef, salt pork, salt fish, butter, cheese, dried peas, ship biscuit, and beer. If the weather was rough, food had to be eaten cold."[7]

The *Arbella* arrived in New England first, after a cold and severe voyage. John Winthrop was possibly its outstanding passenger and wrote of sighting what was later Maine. " 'Then we tacked and stood' " with good weather, fresh and "sweet" air and the odor from the shore was like " 'the smell of a garden.' "[8] The *Arbella* arrived at Salem where its passengers went ashore on June 12, 1630. "There they picked large, sweet wild strawberries, as welcomed change from ship food."[9]

The *Success* came on July 6, 1630. Some of the passengers were almost starved, wrote John Winthrop. The *Talbot* also arrived on July 12, with fourteen of its passengers having died enroute.

The women stayed at Salem while the men searched for a location for settlement. Some few family units already inhabited the area of what is called Boston today. Here the new Puritan immigrants felt they had an appropriate place to locate permanently. On August 23, 1630, "John Winthrop was chosen Governor of the new colony Massachusetts Bay."[10]

NEW HAMPSHIRE (1622)

One of the first steps toward the realization of the colony of New Hampshire came when Reverend John Wheelwright "went north at the beginning of the winter in 1637 and founded Exeter."[1] In 1629 after much wrangling involving John Mason (ardent Anglican) and Sir Ferdinando Gorges, the Mason-Gorges 1622 grant was made and divided. In 1620 the Plymouth Company had revised its plans and obtained a royal charter that created the Council for New England. It should have firmly settled the intermittent wrangling. Instead the Company died.

"So dominant in the Council for New England was Sir Ferdinando Gorges that the Council has been called a 'Gorgeous affair.' "[2] But the council held a title to the entire area of New England, and one way or another it arranged the initial land grant of five colonies—Plymouth, Massachusetts, New Hampshire, Maine, and Connecticut.[3]

The nature of the settlers appears in the hot dissension. Inasmuch as the Council for New England could not deal successfully with the Puritans on fishing rights, Gorges secured the help of Charles I, thereby attempting to get the unquestionable royal authority to replace that of the dead Council. In an effort to implement the King's action "against the Puritans, this Council in 1635 surrendered its rights to function."[4]

In a division of the land grant of August 1622, Mason was recipient of the territory between the Merrimac and Piscataqua Rivers, "which he now called New Hampshire . . ."[5] though for many years in a disputed status."[6] This was perhaps the smallest colony geographically.

Prior to 1860 most of the settlers were either from Great Britain or of British lineage. After the War Between the States, the rapid industrialization and other harbingers of wealth in freedom, migration exploded from all directions geographically and ethnically. Even religious groups who have never known freedom began to seek and thrive on it in America.[7]

Congregationalists were practically a *de facto* "established church." Those not members paid taxes for its upkeep. For most of the decades of the eighteenth century, a non-Congregationalist was ineligible for office. As late as 1819 came the Toleration Act and the cessation of taxing nonmembers to support any church. Only as late as 1876 could those not Protestant qualify to be governor or state senator.[8] Protestant influence ostensibly weakened during the late nineteenth century by the influx of Roman Catholic parishioners from Canada.[9] The American wilderness was blossoming with prosperity and freedom to the extent that all Europe wanted to get in on it, including the Vatican.

NEW YORK (1624)

New York early was and still is one of the most populous states. Waterways, mountains, and geological contour let it dominate as a hinge between New England and the Atlantic seacoast. Cornelius May, the first governor,[1] left Amsterdam in 1623 with thirty families to start a new colony in this Dutch territory. These were Walloon families, robust refugees from Belgium escaping to the Netherlands from religious persecution, as had other Protestants, with Flanders then under Catholic Spain.

In 1664 Charles II named his brother James the Duke of York, proprietor over Dutch lands in the New World.[2] On September 8, 1664, with an English fleet in the harbor of New Amsterdam, the Dutch governor, Peter Stuyvesant, surrendered. Both town and territory were named New York for the royal proprietor.

When Peter Minuit became director general and went to New Amsterdam, he was the first real governor. He sensed accurately that the natural hub of activity was Manhattan Island, for control of the harbor, permanent fortresses, storage, etc. Peter Minuit soon purchased Manahattan from the Indians. On November 3,

66

1626, the company reported to the government of the Netherlands:

> High Mighty Sirs:
> Here arrived today the ship The Arms of Amsterdam which
> sailed from New Netherland out of the Mauritina [Hudson]
> River on September 23; they report that our people there
> are of good courage and live peaceably. Their women also
> have borne children. There, they have bought the Island of
> Manhattan from the wild men for the value of sixty guilders,
> is of 11,000 morgens in extent [a morgen equals about two
> acres]."[3]

The sixty guilders amounted to about twenty-four dollars in
contemporary money, not counting inflation (April 1981). This
was the price of what turned out to be one of the most valuable
pieces of land in the world.

The religion of New Yorkers showed in "dissatisfied English-
men from the New England colonies, Huguenots from France
escaping persecution, and seamen" from many countries.[4]

In 1664 the West India Company chose Peter Stuyvesant as
governor. Stuyvesant had administrative ability, experience in the
West Indies, and a wooden leg strengthened by a plating of silver.
Fellow settlers held him as stubbornly honest and very loyal to
the West India Company.

"A deeply religious man,"[5] he enforced laws strictly, established fire-fighting procedures, founded the first school, built the
first city wharf, and forbade the sale of liquor and firearms to the
Indians. He established a weekly market.

The English based their claims primarily on the work of John
Cabot in 1497, ignoring the papal bulls of 1493. "In 1662,
Charles II revived the English claim to New Netherland. He
granted all of Massachusetts Bay to younger John Winthrop, who
promptly claimed loyalties to date Westchester County as
part of his grant. More important, however, was Charles' gift in
1664 of New Netherland to his brother James, the Duke of York
and Albany."[6] About this time, followed by a "show of force by
Nicholls, Stuyvesant capitulated. New Amsterdam became the

property of the English Crown. . . . The court system was based on that of England and the services of the Church of England were held in the Old Dutch Reform Church. The change from Dutch to English rule was made with very little disturbance to the private and commercial lives of the people."[7]

Religion and morals in New Amsterdam, as it was previously known, were pictured by Pastor Backerus in writing to the Classis of Amsterdam in 1648. He wrote that most of the members of his congregation were generally ignorant of "true religion" and drank heavily. "Seventeen" tap houses were more than adequate to keep this temptation alive for them. If the directors would issue an order for closing all but three or four of these places, the cause of much wickedness and stumbling would disappear. New Amsterdam's population at the time of Pastor Backerus's writing was little more than six hundred.[8]

In 1649 the community had not erected a church. In 1654 Dutch clergymen and churches were found only in New Amsterdam, Albany, and in some two of the Patroonships. The people who worshipped at New Amsterdam had to travel as much as three hours in order to arrive for worship. By 1664 more improvements began to take place. By the time the English had taken over, twelve Dutch Reform churches graced the colonies.

In this heterogeneous congregation one pastor observed "Papists, Mennonites and Lutherans among the Dutch."[9] He added that there were also numerous Puritans or Independents, numerous atheists, and "various other servants of Baal among the English under this government, who concealed themselves under the name of Christians."[10] The area had a number of Jews.

Anglicans had only one chapel in 1676. It became an established church in 1693. At that time it had services in the four counties of New York, Westchester, Queens, and Richmond. Some Congregational churches were in eastern Long Island and at an English town. Even the Lutherans had two churches by 1668. The Swedish Lutherans clustered in the Delaware region and had four strongly established churches until as late as 1682. Governor Andros said of New York in 1678 that it had twenty-four towns and "religions of all sorts—one church of England, several Protestants and Independents, Quakers, Anabaptists of several sects, some Jews, but Presbyterians and Independents most numerous and substantial."[11]

CONNECTICUT (1635)

Connecticut was an outgrowth of Massachusetts, with Quakers early dominating while the idealism of William Penn reached out like the roots of a great tree. The settlers of Connecticut left Massachusetts freely and in "good religious standing." Several towns on the river, the Hartford section, were thriving by 1636.

In 1677 Massachusetts, "the Holy Experiment,"[1] purchased the claims of the Gorges heirs, gaining control of future Maine. New Hampshire became a royal province in 1679.

New Englanders won the Pequot War of 1637. But the continued Indian warfare lost them many towns and settlers. Security came only as the colonies united in "The England Confederation."[2]

In 1634 some followers of Thomas Hooker (New Town) secured permission to transfer to the Connecticut valley. In May 1635 they received a grant as original petitioners (also for the dwellers of Watertown, Roxbury, and Dorchester) to transfer wherever they wanted to provided they continue under the governmental umbrella of Massachusetts.

The transfer began in 1635 and continued for a year. They drove their cattle and went "hacking their laborious way through the New England forest."[3] They plodded their way to what they regarded as the promised land, establishing themselves in Hartford, Windsor, and Weathersfield on the river. Rev. Thomas Hooker reached this same destination in 1636 and settled in Hartford, which later became the capital of the colony.

Winning out with the Indians (Pequot War) placed the Connecticut people on the level of sovereignty with prominent government organizations from within. Thus Rev. Thomas Hooker, on May 31, 1638, gave expression to the political tenets of Connecticut in a now famous sermon. "The foundation of authority," he said, "is laid . . . in the free consent of the people, to whom belongs the choice of public magistrates by God's own allowance." The three towns then adopted a governmental pattern on this principle, officially in January 1639 called the now-famous "Fundamental Order of Connecticut."

"This charter of the 'people' declared the purpose of forming a confederation to preserve the purity of the Gospel and the discipline of the churches, and to provide laws for a civil government."[4]

MARYLAND (1634)

Only one Roman Catholic signed the Declaration of Independence. Was this good or bad? For whom? Good if Carroll's compatriots back him on what he signed about religion. He is Charles Carroll, one of our all-time favorite Roman Catholic heroes. (See the *Signers of the Declaration of Independence*, by Katherine and John Bakeless, pub. Houghton Mifflin Company, Boston, pp. 233-247.)

But Anson Phelps Stokes[1] explains why he raises Carroll to a seat among the immortals: "With the inherited tradition of his church, whose members conscientiously believe that they are the only true church of Christ, it has not always been easy for Catholics to advocate complete religious freedom, especially in Catholic countries. Many doubted whether they could identify themselves consistently with a movement for such freedom in the United States. [Although] Rev. John Carroll's specific utterances on the subject are not many . . . as the leading Catholic priest in the colonies, he believed in the Revolutionary cause; he was a staunch supporter of the Constitution with its religious freedom guarantees; and an advocate of an American selected Hierarchy . . . and of a church adjusted to the needs of a democratic nation."[2]

Serious questions hover over opposition to "an American selected hierarchy" (by American Catholics, of course). If the hierarchy is not selected by American Catholics, many American compatriots are in effect acceding to the preference of a foreign state (the Vatican), which already wants a most basic aspect of the United States Constitution changed. This posture by either the esteemed British Parliament, the unyielding Kremlin of Moscow, or the Italian (over sixty percent) Vatican of Rome, is not always consonant with America's interests. Why wouldn't Catholics outside America trust American Catholics to elect their own bishops or archbishops? Since they do not trust them, and they are the only worldwide religious fellowship that does not trust their American sector (wing, segment, archbishopric, operation), why should others? Would the United States permit a labor union to have officials approved only by Italy, Russia, or China? A Catholic official approved ultimately only by a foreign state (the Vatican) is not consonant with American constitutionalism. When the American hierarchy is active and uses its influence regarding taxes, election of officials (e.g., Mr. Ted Kennedy), foreign policy, it ought to be chosen by American Catholics. Catholic Von Papen remained in Hitler's cabinet toward the last—just in the unlikely event that Germany . . .

The sole Romanist to sign the Declaration of Independence was Hon. Charles Carroll of Carrollton. We and his coreligionists owe it to him to be true to that declaration and to the Constitution that grew out of the Declaration. For his subsequent coreligionists not to support him in perpetuity raises the question of the jesuitical principle of "the ends justifies the means."

The United States, on acceding to ecclesiastical absolutism, arrogance, or pride creates one loophole of potential danger to its security and policies.

It is unfortunate that Carroll's successors have not seen fit to pursue his attitude. Had they done so, there would not now be any Roman Catholic problem regarding government support for parochial schools in this country.[3] The issue of public support for any but public schools would not be as confusing as it is.

Through schools, adults can teach children religious ideas from which mature minds logically and intelligently recoil. By clever pedagogy men can put nonsense on stilts. True religious liberty projects the privilege of being nonreligious or nonsupportive of a given religion as well as freedom to be religious.

There were many Carrolls. To help identify himself this one usually referred to himself as "Charles Carroll of Carrollton."[4]

His grandfather had come from a noble family of Irishmen who had arrived in Maryland in late 1688 and was attorney-general of the colony (called a province then). The Carrolls had migrated to Maryland at this time because they were Catholics and had been subjected to the religious tensions of England since the time of Henry VIII.

Lord Baltimore was a Catholic who had established the colony in about 1634. He nobly designed it as a place of refuge for his fellow Catholics and also for peoples of other sects who were persecuted. By the time the son of the attorney-general, namely Charles Carroll from Annapolis, was grown, the Protestants of Maryland had transferred their suspicions and fear of political propensities of the Roman Catholic Church to their new homeland and had a kind of discrimination that infuriated the Charles Carroll of Annapolis, who turned out to be the father of the sole Roman Catholic signer of the Declaration of Independence.

"Maryland, where a Catholic minority ruled a Protestant majority twenty times its size,"[5] just may have gained more than she lost from the changes in British rulers during this period. "The Catholic proprietor's 'partiality . . . towards those of the Popish Religion' gave Catholics a monopoly of 'the highest places of trust, profit, and honor.' Quarrels over the exercise of the veto power, legislative apportionment, a favoritism in land grants, and regulation of the tobacco trade supplemented the religious issue in augmenting the discontent which had produced three earlier insurrections in 1659, 1676, and 1681."[6]

The revolutionaries liked it when William and Mary changed Maryland into a province of the crown. This removed state power over the colony from the Calverts but did not touch their real estate holdings. Meanwhile, Benedict Calvert accepted the Anglican faith and George I restored his proprietorship. The Anglican Church ironically became the "state church" of Maryland in 1702!

During the time that Virginia was slowly becoming a strong colony, just north of it the new colony of Maryland was beginning. In 1632 Sir George Calvert, First Lord Baltimore, secured from Charles I formal control of the land.[7] Here the first contingent of Catholic believers came on May 25, 1634.

The manorial families were for the most part Catholic. Catholics did not ever outnumber others but remained a minority in Maryland. They and the established churches of England conducted separate worship. Lord Baltimore refused to permit any Jesuits in the colony to circumscribe Protestants or impose any limits on them. The well-known Maryland Toleration Act of 1649, assuring the liberty in church services to Christians of all faiths, was of Lord Baltimore's leadership. This was far from American freedom: unbelievers, or those not Christian, were subject to execution! The Act at least was progress toward liberty of conscience.[8] Execution was for nontrinitarians! Maryland's tolerance was better than Europe's stake-burning intolerance. The American pattern of liberty which prevailed probably evolved in Rhode Island.

Maryland's Act of Toleration was a policy of enlightened self-interest. Her few Catholics were surrounded by Protestants in every direction. Most Protestants bore deep feelings about the tight, monolithic, monstrously poised, ecclesiastical entity of Italy, together with the attested burnings of dissidents at the stake. All this made a concession of religious tolerance by Catholics wise, if not indispensable.

Toleration, religious or racial, is basically denigrating if not actually insulting. "I'll put up with you in spite of my revulsion for you" is its tone whether expressed or not. But Christ taught, "By this shall all men know that you are my disciples, if you have love one for another" (John 13:35, Douay Version).

"The triumph of the Puritans in the English Civil War further exposed the proprietor to attack. Accordingly, in 1648 Lord Baltimore appointed a Protestant governor and sent over to the colony a bill that became the famous Toleration Act of 1649. (It guaranteed freedom of conscience to all Christians who respected the rights of the proprietor!) Any person who disturbed a Christian in his chosen worship should pay treble damages and a fine of twenty shillings.

"Except for a brief period, 1654-58, the Toleration Act of 1649 guided the religious policy of the proprietors, and as a result the radical Protestants multiplied until they accounted for three-fourths of the population, as against a sixth who were Anglicans and a twelfth of the government of Maryland. The Anglican Church was officially established in 1692, but it did not attain the supremacy which it enjoyed in Virginia."[9]

RHODE ISLAND (1636)

Some refer to Rhode Island as the colony that was "small in size, large in history."[1] Its history delineates clearly the differences among religious toleration, religious liberty, and a free church in a free state.[2] Toleration condescends to "put up" with other beliefs and churches. Religious liberty is freedom to share one's faith with others who are willing to hear. Religion in a school curriculum uses requirements or a form of force. If the government pays any part, it is the nation enforcing religious instruction. A free church in a free state assumes each to be sovereign in its sphere. Unfair or subtle methods of "getting a hearing" or gaining prestigious advantages by direct or indirect state support alters the liberty of others. Since education is either required or assumed, for a school teaching religion to receive direct or indirect government support violates the principle and the Constitution: "Congress shall make no law respecting an establishment of religion . . ." Income tax deductions for tuition payments to either Protestant or non-Protestant schools puts the government in the business of religion. To have ambassadorial exchanges with a religion (as the Vatican), which is also a state, gives one religion prestige over one not formally in politics. It is majoring on politics and subordinating spiritual values to "statecraft" firstly.

Only Rhode Island originated in America. The other twelve were conceived or chartered in the Old World. The Reverend Roger Williams led in founding Rhode Island in 1636. The colony achieved statehood in 1790. Its size totals 1,214 square miles with 1,058 miles inland and 156 in water. Georgia could have contained it almost fifty times.

This colony has a reputation for some bad as well as some good characteristics. It was the last to sign the Declaration of Independence and join in the Revolution. It had already challenged Great Britain by violent resistances: its men destroyed the British revenue ship *Liberty* in 1769; they burned the British revenue schooner, *Gaspee*, in 1772. One of the most vicious battles of King Philip's war with the Indians occurred on Rhode Island soil. The area was notorious for the pirates that hid out on its soil, including the legendary "success," Captain Kidd, in this dubious profession.

Roger Williams was strongly of the conviction that state and church should each be free of the other and each sovereign in its own sphere. Authorities of government were never justified in punishing church members for the infraction of requirements or regulations of church or religion. One of his firmest convictions had to do with liberty of conscience. He also took the position that the king of England had no right to give away the land that was the property of the Indians.

For these reasons and in view of his unwillingness to subscribe to the oath required of the residents of Massachusetts, Williams received an order to return to England. The authorities decided, however, to give him permission to stay in the Bay Colony until the following spring if he would not preach the aforementioned convictions. He could not hold his peace. When he learned that the officers were coming to arrest him, he left Salem. He avoided arrest only by a few hours. His wife opened the door for the law officers, while holding in her arms her baby just born and named "Freeborn."

When he fled he made for the headquarters of Massasoit, the famous Indian chieftain. Rhode Island at one time was the largest center for slavery buying and selling in the new world.

The first official name of Rhode Island as a colony was "The Incorporation of Providence Plantations in the Narragansett Bay in New England." Until this day Rhode Island claims the exclusive name "The State of Rhode Island and Providence Plantations."[3]

Roger Williams mastered an Indian dialect, produced a lexicon for Indian-English, and was described by an acquaintance as "the sweetest soul I ever knew."[4]

"God," he would later write in a pamphlet war with his Puritan adversaries, "requireth not a uniformity of religion to be . . . enforced in any civil state; which enforced uniformity . . . is greatest occasion of civil war, . . . persecution, . . . and . . . hypocrisy."[5] He secured a charter as a result of the largesse of Parliament in 1664 in order to restrain the potential aggressiveness of Massachusetts. He made sure that it accorded residents "freedom of conscience and separation of church and state as well as representative government."[6]

A Hebrew, Oscar St. Straus, who just may have done as much research on the beginnings of the basic principles of life and freedom in the United States as anyone, has observed that Roger Williams was possibly the "real founder of the new Republic," which Republic continues as the best time-tested instance of democracy in the history of humanity up until now. He adds that the "separate church and state" concept began at Providence, Rhode Island. A religious liberty that appeals to the Hebrew mind, in view of long Jewish exposure to the widest variety of persecutions, should have something substantive.

More biographies of Roger Williams have now appeared and are still within reach of Americans than the biographies of any other early American prior to Benjamin Franklin.

Generations ago some labeled the Puritans as people who came to this country chiefly to catch fish instead of "Praise God." The historical background and achievements of Puritans show that they settled the country with stability as few newcomers did, that they excelled in agriculture and industry eventually, and that they made excellent citizens. Their tendency to "Praise God"[7] has been a healthy antidote to some of a not-so-praiseful tendency, and even some whose demeanor would multiply the social, moral, and economic problems of the country. The Puritans "spun off" at least "three other New England colonies."[8]

RELIGIOUS DIVERSITY IN RHODE ISLAND

Anglicans and Congregationalists also founded significant churches in Rhode Island. Still late, its tolerance made it a colonial center of Judaism, and eventually it came to have more Roman Catholics in proportion to its population than any other state in the Union.

DELAWARE (1638)

Geographically, Delaware came out of New Netherland (New York), and the first permanent settlements were founded in 1638. It became a proprietary colony of William Penn, zealous founder of Quakerism. Delaware, chartered in 1681, may have settled a debt Charles II "owed" Penn's father, a navy admiral and rich landholder.

"Lutheranism was designated by The South Company as the official religion although toleration was extended to Calvinists of the Dutch Reform Church."[1]

Quaker beliefs, strong in Rhode Island, New Jersey, and North Carolina, were the life in Penn's colonies. "Quaker" originated as derision that one should "tremble or quake at mention of God."[2] Officially, members were "Friends." George Fox, a former shoemaker's apprentice from Nottingham, started Quakerism during the religious turmoil of the English Civil War (1647). He affirmed that spiritual authority did not exist in a visible church nor even in Scripture, but in an "inner light" from the Lord to each seeker. This radical departure from sacerdotal Catholicism and infantile dependence on priests generated rigorous commitment to egalitarianism. One man's inner light was apt to be as accurate as another's. Quakers chose no clergy to be remunerated. They listened sincerely to any brother or sister if he (or she) seemed moved to articulate divine communications in meetings shorn of all ceremony.

Plain clothing, no hat tipping to superiors, addressing others by "thee" and "thou" made for egalitarianism. Pacifism was strong. Aggressive in proselytizing, they often landed in detention. A few were executed; many were scourged.

Penn, a Quaker missionary, was incarcerated more than once because of extremism. He wanted Massachusetts and Delaware to be a "Holy Experiment," an asylum for Quakers, potential martyrs, and for others subjected to persecution for faith.[2]

Delaware basically was founded by Swedes and Dutch. Religious inclinations included Dutch Reform mingled with the Lutheranism of the Swedes.

Delaware was deeded to William Penn in 1682. By 1788 it was one of the early five colonies to ratify the Constitution with a strong statement on freedom of religion. Peter Riddy, then governor in place of Minuit, carried along additional settlers, including two preachers to Delaware.[3] The colony's name came from Lord De La Wara, one of the earliest settlers in Virginia, "a privy councillor under both Elizabeth I and James I."[4] Until 1701 Delaware was a part of Pennsylvania.

Swedish Lutherans put up and sustained its earliest churches from about 1638. Wilmington could boast of a log chapel even then. Reverend John Yeo, able exponent for an "established" ministry in Maryland, left for New Castle (Delaware) and, with the concurrence of the governor, became the designated minister for the Delaware area. The people, gradually spanning the cultural gaps, were absorbed into the Anglican tradition. "The Old Swedes" (Trinity) Church in Wilmington, erected in 1698, abandoned the Swedish language in the next century and, along with the Old Swedes' (Gloria Dei) Church of Philadelphis and a few other Swedish congregations, gradually became Anglican."[5] The Dutch Reform Church was decisively the major religious influence, supplemented by the Swedish colony, which was Lutheran. It gradually merged with the Anglican Church.

"Congregationalism was the major religious influence in New England."[6]

PENNSYLVANIA (1643)

Pennsylvania was early called the "Keystone State," "because of its pivotal place" between "the adjacent and nearby colonies both above and below it to the north and south."[1] Its motto was

"Virtue, liberty, and independence." Long hospitable to all creeds, "It proclaimed 'liberty' when the Declaration of Independence was framed in the colony's largest city, Philadelphia (from the Greek *philo,* or love, and *adelphos,* or brother) and was known as the city of brotherly love."[2]

A stone called "boundary stone" identified the Mason-Dixon Line and separated Pennsylvania from Maryland. Thus the stones extended for several miles, "every fifth one showing the arms of Penn on the one side and the arms of Lord Baltimore on the other."[3] The word *sylvan,* or "forest" in Latin, was added to "Penn" to form the name *Pennsylvania.*

Its earlier history is tied indissolubly with the faith, ideology, and life of William Penn (1644-1718). His father was the great Admiral Penn. Young Penn was a student at Christ Church (Oxford), Saumur, and Lincoln's Inn.[3] He denounced Oxford (usually regarded as a good school by any standards) and other English universities as single places of idleness, looseness, profaneness, prodigality, and "gross ignorance." He was expelled for religious nonconformity in 1662. The turbulance of that age had extended to matters of religion. The Church of England had been created in a split from the Roman Catholic Church during the reign of Henry VIII (1509-1547). The King of England was now head of both state and church.

In his teens young William Penn asked questions about religion that children of higher classes were not supposed to ask. He was a friend of the Duke of York, a Catholic, and manager of his father's Irish estate. He traveled widely.

William Penn was deeply spiritual, committed to the principles of Quakerism from his youth. Penn believed that religion was a matter of individual conscience. Young Penn went so far as to assert that man could communicate with God directly and that mediation of the clergy was unnecessary. No man was better fitted to undertake a colonial venture whose express purpose was to provide a sanctuary for the persecuted people of Europe.

Particularly disturbed by the disabilities imposed on his fellow Quakers, he began after 1679 to lose his confidence in England;

and, like John Winthrop a half century before, he set his eyes and hopes on the New World.

Few early Americans have made as deep and lasting a contribution to the character of American manhood as William Penn. For his vast, rich, inland domain, Penn provided a full set of laws, "a code of Quaker principles applied to actual government." The frame of government called for a resident governor, a small elective council, and a large elective assembly with very limited powers. The franchise was restricted to men with land and property. Preferential treatment for Anglicans was nominally exacted by the charter, but freedom of worship was assured for all who believed in God.[3]

NORTH CAROLINA (1653)

At first Spain was the most tenacious nation attempting exploration and settlement in the North Carolina region. And Spain had the papal *bullas* of 1493 to back her. The pope ruled that only Spaniards and Portuguese could settle there (see ch. four). In 1520 Pedro de Quexois went from Santo Domingo to the general area of the Carolinas,[1] and led an effort that ended in failure. Also Spanish official, explorer, and slave trader Luiz Vazquez de Ayllon in July 1526 led over 500 men, women, and children, several black slaves, and ninety horses into the area, penetrated the Rio Jordan, and started a colony at what was known later as Cape Fear. This colony failed in a story of betrayal, mutiny, disease and disillusionment. The surviving members (only 150) returned to Santo Domingo at Ayllon's death, October 18. In 1540 Hernando de Soto went on his well-known search for hills yielding an abundance of gold.[2] Indians had persisted in stories of gold abounding in the north.

On April 9, 1585, Raleigh went out to establish the first English colony in the New World. He had a fleet of seven ships that were stocked for a long trip, and carried both sailors and colonists. There were 108 men, with no women or children, who sailed from

Plymouth on April 9, 1585. Their commander was Sir Richard Grenville, a cousin of Raleigh's. Ralph Lane was their lieutenant governor.

Thomas Harriot was a preacher, scientist, and instructor of Raleigh's in mathematics. Thomas Cavendish was the "boy wonder," who later circumnavigated the whole world. This Grenville expedition arrived in 1586. Other ships with supplies and more men arrived intermittently. Grenville searched without success for previous settlers. He finally left for England, leaving eighteen men equipped adequately to endure at least two years,[3] with a view to retaining the claim of England to this land.

Shortly after The Colony led by John White[4] (with 110 settlers including 17 women and 9 children) arrived off Hatteras July 22, 1587, two significant events occurred. First Manteo, known as a docile and free Indian, accepted baptism, which was the first Protestant (1587) service of this kind known to have taken place in the New World. Second Virginia Dare was born on August 18, the daughter of Annanias and Eleanor White Dare. She in turn was the granddaughter of Governor White, and was the first child born to English parents in America.

The territory now called North Carolina and the Albemarle Sound regions were earlier a part of the Virginia charter boundary of 1606 and the expanded grant of 1609.

Rigidity in Virginia's established church (Anglican) may have helped North Carolina. One result of Virginia's early tight laws against nonconformity was a gradual removal of dissenters to neighboring areas, including the Albermarle Sound region, which ultimately became North Carolina. Quakers apparently were the most numerous; and when they were not temporarily outmaneuvered or disqualified, they played a significant role later in the assembly.

George Fox was the first missionary of any group in North Carolina. He spent a month among these people in 1672, healing the wife of a former governor, holding a disputation in another governor's house, visiting many Friends, and conducting several meetings.

Baptists, Presbyterians, and some New England Puritans moved in. The North Carolina Assembly passed an act establishing the Anglican Church in 1701. The settlers vigorously protested this and the proprietors quickly disqualified it. In 1705, after Quaker members of the assembly had been expelled, a Vestry Act was passed. It too was nullified (by Carey's Rebellion), and was not restored until 1741. By that time life in North Carolina had become settled, and the royal government was as firmly in power as it could be in a land of many uprisings.

French Huguenots from Virginia then began to locate in the colony rapidly. Many of the new settlers came from Manakin Town, a French Huguenot community near the future site of Richmond. Expecting to avoid persecution in France, the Huguenots began this community in 1700, led by Marquis de la Muce and Charles de Sailly.

Earlier, in 1690-1691, while Thomas Jarvis was "acting governor," the proprietors in London assigned Ludwell to be "Governor of Carolina" (North and South). Charles Towne (in the southern part of Carolina) was in effect the capital city. Since those in the northern part of Carolina found it difficult to go to Charles Towne, the division into North and South may have been forthcoming early. So two great colonies parted and later became two great states.

NEW JERSEY (1660)

Like a large sandwich filling between two huge colonies, New Jersey was like a main road with a place to stop between New York City and Philadelphia. It was more "a neat place to go through but not a place to stay."[1] No matter how rapidly or in what ways New Jersey continued to grow, it never outgrew its two neighbors and was always like a plant in the shade of its "powerful neighbors to the east and west."[2]

Those ultimately "choosing" New Jersey often simply flowed

over from one of the two major neighboring colonies. Thus New Jersey received a host of "tolerant Quakers from Pennsylvania in the west, hard-shelled Puritans from New England in the east, mercantile-oriented Dutch in the north (Dutch Reform Church usually), farming Swedes (usually Lutherans) in the south."[3]

New Jersey became the ninth of the thirteen colonies in 1664. Jersey is a small island near the western coast of France. George Carteret had held the enemies of Jersey Island at bay for some time and supplied its defense during the British Civil War (1642). King Charles II knighted him for this and assigned him some yet-to-be-specified land in the New World. The Duke of York then gave the land between the Hudson and Delaware Rivers to Sir George Carteret and Lord John Berkeley.

The settlers brought a society pervaded by Quaker piety and sobriety. From them emerged in the eighteenth century two of America's greatest Quaker leaders, John Wooman and Stephen Grellet.

The proprietors projected "The Concessions and Agreements of the Lords Proprietors of the Province of Nova Caesarea of New Jersey" in February 29, 1665. It guaranteed religious freedom and permission for the proprietors to choose the governor.

After this the English settlers coming to New Jersey in great numbers were mostly Puritans from New England and Long Island. They had come to the Western world because of their penchant for strictness and simplicity of life and for worshipping God. At this time Britons were persecuting Quakers in England. Accordingly, many Quakers welcomed a refuge in the New World.[4]

The Quaker trustees who had purchased Berkeley's part of New Jersey reached a concord with George Carteret on July 1, 1676. This involved splitting the colony into two portions; the Quakers overran West Jersey with settlements and this portion covered about 4,600 square miles. East Jersey included about 3,000 square miles and belonged to Carteret. The two together were slightly less than the size of modern Palestine in 1947 at the time of partition. The farms of East Jersey were usually small.

The inhabitants were mostly Presbyterian, Dutch Reformed, Baptist, and Anglican.

SOUTH CAROLINA (1670)

South Carolina, founded in 1670, early had far more dissenters than members of established churches. William Sayle, the first governor, was a Puritan. Some of the ninety-three who migrated to South Carolina with him may have been of strong Baptist leanings. In 1683 Lord Cardross started a settlement of Scotsmen. They too had Baptist leanings, as did a group from Somersetshire under the leadership of Humphrey Blake (1682-83). An aggregation of Baptists from Kittery, Maine, arrived about this time. By 1700 Charleston had a strong Baptist congregation.

A sizable band of Huguenots began and organized in 1680. Quakers, rapidly increasing, supplied the budding colony with a governor, John Archdale (in office 1694-1695). The numerical size of these groups did not compensate for the lack of strength of these widely dispersed believers. They had strength that they had not yet learned to harness. The future of these dedicated immigrants would glow with yet-to-come immigration, biblical revivals, spiritual awakenings, and external organizational revivals.

South Carolina's immigrants were often small-time planters pressured out of overpopulated Barbados, cultured Protestant refugees (Huguenots) from France, and immigrants from England with capital and close ties with leaders. There were also New Englanders. The unusually good harbor of Charles Towne—Charleston—conduced to the acquisition of maritime commerce. Charles Towne for a while was located some distance down river from its present location (1670). Some ten years later it was returned.

Exports of staple and lumber to the West Indies and of hides and furs to Britain comprised the bulk of the shipping. South Carolina before 1700 was able to begin exporting rice grown on the colony's plantations. From early times the population was decidely aristocratic. The people to the north were sturdy, strong, plodding, dependable. Those to the south were more enterprising. Two different types of people, not levels, became (1712) self-evident, resulting in a separate government for North Carolina.[2]

In South Carolina the dissidents readily achieved a way of living with the Anglican Church. "The first church in Charleston, Saint Philip's, was built in 1681 of black cypress on a brick foundation. Atkin Williamson served it until 1696, when Samuel Marshall replaced him as rector. By 1723 there were thirteen parishes; and those in the more populous areas were fairly prosperous, boasting substantial buildings, comfortable parsonages, glebes [land belonging or yielding revenues to a chapel or ecclesiastical institution] of several hundred acres, and governmental guarantees of support."[3]

In less accessible areas, the churches occasionally suffered for lack of a pastor. "The office of Commissary of the Bishop of London was established in 1707, and was usually occupied by men of energy and sagacity."[4]

Through ministers whom he alone appointed, the king commanded the armed forces, conducted diplomacy, and appointed people not only to all civil, military and judicial offices but to those in the Anglican Church as well. He also handled all monetary expenditures, and decided when, whether and for what duration Parliament could assemble. Any planned recalcitrance was almost equal to "disloyalty." In keeping with the Anglican teaching of nonresistance, most communicants seldom did other than accede to the preferences or even whims of the king.

The House of Lords and the House of Commons seldom experienced equality in strength. The House of Lords, composed of men of inherited titles *and Anglican bishops,* had largely a dubious part: on monetary issues it could not even amend. "It had to accept or reject what the elected House of Commons arranged. Nobles who sat in the House of Lords, however, were very often major ministers (administrative officers) of the Crown and in the same capacity as the political leaders who managed the Commons."[5]

The colony was Protestant and evangelical, even though encumbered by an established church. Its people of faith and refinement soon moved into the evangelical midstream.

GEORGIA (1733)

English leaders established Georgia in 1733 as (1) an extension of the southern frontier as a buffer between the Florida (then Spanish) and the English settlements; (2) a planned Utopia or model society; (3) a refuge for persecuted European Protestants; (4) a new opportunity for men released from English debtors' prisons; and (5) a model colony to produce commodities for England, notably silk and citrus fruits.

Georgia was a part of the earlier Carolina grant, but fear of the Spanish in Florida (who destroyed an approaching settlement in 1686)[1] delayed its beginning for half a century. General James Oglethorpe began it in 1732. Having fought against the Spanish, he wanted a military bastion to contain them decisively in Florida. Leading a parliamentary investigation, Oglethorpe learned of the noncriminal debtors pining away in English jails. He wanted to give them a new start and strengthen his plans for a military stronghold by settling them as farmers and militiamen in Georgia. The king thus conferred the land upon him and nineteen others as proprietary trustees for twenty-one years.

The Protestants of Germany about this time were being persecuted vigorously and needed protection.

Both John Wesley, who founded Methodism, and George Whitfield resided in Georgia for some time. Whitfield established the first home for orphans in the colonies, near Savannah.

The overwhelming majority of settlers by 1689 had come from English stock. The largest non-English group were the negroes, over 200,000, with nine-tenths situated in the south. Next in volume were the Scotch-Irish; then the Germans, Irish, Scotch, and the French Huguenots, who were among the most vigorous and talented of Protestants. Small collections came from Switzerland and Scandanavia, Jews from all areas of the globe.[2]

VARYING MOTIVATIONS FOR MIGRATING TO THE WESTERN HEMISPHERE

A chief phenomenon of this general period was persecution of all dissenters by state churches. This "church" so mercilessly and persistently persecuted the dissenters that the persecuted ones longed for almost any haven of relief. The persecuted were usually Protestants or dissenters disagreeing with the state churches.

When some Protestant wing came into ascendancy temporarily, as was true intermittently in England, for example, Roman Catholics were persecuted. In fact the genius of United States history ultimately stemmed from the fact that England became Protestant and decisively won out in the part of North America that became the United States. This in part explains how it happens that one, though only one, of the original thirteen colonies that composed the United States, began as a Catholic colony even though its Protestants outnumbered others twenty to one. This was Maryland. The study of this and all other colonies in their striving, growing, organizing, and achieving statehood is one of the romances of all time.

A major difference between settlers of North America and those of South America was that those of the South were seeking *gold* while those of the North were seeking *God* and freedom to serve Him. Regardless of how literally true this was or not, one will find below some nineteen citations in which some eleven historians have made similar observations in varying language or give hardcore historical examples of the principle dramatized on the spot.

Regardless of the degree to which gold was a motive in those settlements in North America and South America, those of North America have a serious problem. Understandably they must solve their social problems. They find it difficult to keep the profit motive from becoming an obsessive way of life to all instead of a healthy but collectively disciplined motive for sustaining a robust economy fair to all citizens. As overly pious and stereotyped as it may sound, democracy cannot survive without good people.

Notes

INTRODUCTION

1. *The World Book Encyclopedia* Vol. 4, World Book—Child-Craft International, Inc., Chicago, 1978 edition, p. 632.

VIRGINIA

1. Sydney E. Ahlstrom, *A Religious History of the American People*, Yale University Press, New Haven, 1972, p. 104.
2. Ibid., p. 105.
3. Curtis P. Nettles, *The Roots of American Civilization*, Appleton-Century-Croft, New York, Division of Meredith Publishing Co., 1963, p. 110.
4. Ibid., p. 110.
5. *The Democratic Experience*, Third Edition, Carl N. Degler, Thomas C. Cochran, Vincent P. DeSantis, Holman Hamilton, William H. Harbaugh, Arthur S. Link, Russell B. Nye, David Potter, Clarence L. Versteeg, 1973, Scott, Foresman and Company, Glenview, Ill., p. 12.
6. Sidney E. Ahlstrom, *A Religious History of the American People*, Yale University Press, New Haven, 1972, pp. 193-196, 339.

MASSACHUSETTS

1. *A History of the United States*, volume 1, Norman A. Graebner, Gilbert C. Fite, Phillip L. White, 1970, McGraw-Hill Book Company, New York, p. 50.
2. Ibid., p. 50.
3. Ibid., p. 50-51.

4. Alice Dickinson, *The Colony of Massachusetts*, 1975, Franklin Watts, Inc., p. 4.

5. Ibid., p. 4.

6. Ibid., p. 7.

7. Ibid., p. 9.

8. Ibid., p. 9.

9. Ibid., p. 9.

10. Ibid., p. 11.

NEW HAMPSHIRE

1. Curtis P. Nettles, *The Roots of American Civilization—A History of American Colonial Life*, Appleton-Century-Crofts, 1963, New York, p. 179.

2. Ibid., p. 114.

3. Ibid., p. 115.

4. Ibid., p. 115.

5. Ibid., p. 115.

6. *A History of the United States*, vol. 1, Norman A. Graebner, Gilbert C. Fite, Phillip L. White, 1970, McGraw-Hill Book Company, New York, p. 61.

7. *American Encyclopedia*, vol. 20, p. 172.

8. Marcus Wilson Jernegan, *The American Colonies 1492-1750*, Frederick Ungar Publishing Company, New York, p. 137-138.

9. Ibid., p. 173.

NEW YORK

1. David Goodnough, *The Colony of New York*, c. 1973, Franklin Watts, Inc., Franklin Watts, New York, p. 2.

2. Ibid., p. 5.

3. Ibid., p. 16.

4. Ibid., p. 16.

5. Ibid., p. 16.

6. Curtis P. Nettles, *The Roots of American Civilization*, Appleton-Century-Crofts, Division of Meredith Publishing Company, 1963, p. 127.

7. *The Democratic Experience*, Third Edition, Degler, Cochran, DeSantis, Hamilton, Harbaugh, Link, Nye, etc. Scott Foresman and Co., Glenview, Ill., 1973, p. 15.

8. David Goodnough, *The Colony of New York*, c. 1973, Franklin Watts, Inc., Franklin Watts, New York, p. 19.

9. Ibid., p. 21.
10. Ibid., p. 36.
11. Ibid., p. 40.

CONNECTICUT

1. *A History of the United States,* Vol. 1, McGraw-Hill Book Company, New York, 1970, p. 52.
2. Ibid., p. 61.
3. Curtis P. Nettles, *The Roots of American Civilization,* Second Edition, Appleton-Century-Crofts, New York, 1973, p. 173.
4. Sidney E. Ahlstrom, *A Religious History of the American People,* Yale University Press, New Haven, 1972, p. 99.

MARYLAND

1. Anson Phelps Stokes, *Church and State in the United States,* Harper & Row Publishers, New York, pp. 30-63; 64-82; 104ff.
2. Joseph Martin Dawson, *Baptists and the American Republic,* Broadman Press, Nashville, Tennessee, 1956, p. 9.
3. Ibid., p. 10.
4. Katherine and John Bakeless, *Signers of the Declaration,* Houghton Mifflin Co., Boston, 1969, p. 233.
5. *A History of the United States,* Vol. 1, Norman A. Graebner, Gilbert C. Fite, Phillip L. White, McGraw-Hill Book Company, New York, p. 137.
6. Ibid., pp. 137-139.
7. *The Democratic Experience,* Third Edition, Carl N. Degler, Thomas C. Cochran, Vincent P. DeSantis, Holman Hamilton, William H. Harbaugh, Arthur S. Link, Russell B. Nye, David M. Potter, Clarence L. VerSteeg, Scott, Foresman and Company, Glenview, Ill., p. 14.
8. Ibid., p. 14-15.
9. Curtis P. Nettles, *The Roots of American Civilization,* Second Edition, Appleton-Century-Crofts, Division of Meredith Publishing Company, New York, p. 186.

RHODE ISLAND

1. Robert N. Webb, *The Colony of Rhode Island,* Franklin Watts, Inc., New York, 1972, p. 3.

2. Ibid., p. 4.
3. Ibid., p. 5.
4. Ibid., p. 10.
5. Ibid., p. 13.
6. *History of the United States*, Vol. 1, Norman A. Graebner, Gilbert C. Fite, Phillip L. White; McGraw-Hill Book Company, 1970, p. 52.
7. James Hastings Nichols, *Democracy and the Churches*, Westminister Press, Philadelphia, p. 29.
8. *History of the United States*, Vol. 1, Norman A. Graebner, Gilbert C. Fite, Phillip L. White, McGraw-Hill Book Company, 1970, p. 51.

DELAWARE

1. *The Roots of American Civilization, A History of American Colonial Life*, Second Edition, Appleton-Century-Crofts, New York, 1964, p. 200.
2. *A History of the United States*, Norman A. Graebner, Gilbert C. Fite, Phillip L. White, McGraw-Hill Book Company, New York, 1970, Vol. 1, p. 66-67.
3. John E. Pomfret and Floyd H. Shumway, *Founding the American Colonies*, Harper & Row Publishers, New York, p. 293.
4. Sidney E. Ahlstrom, *A Religious History of the American People*, Yale University Press, New Haven, 1972, p. 216.
5. Ibid., p. 217.
6. *A History of the United States*, Norman A. Graebner, Gilbert C. Fite, Phillip L. White, McGraw-Hill Book Company, New York, 1970, Vol. 1, p. 128.

PENNSYLVANIA

1. Emil Lengyel, *The Colony of Pennsylvania*, Franklin Watts, Inc., New York, 1974, p. 1.
2. Ibid., p. 2.
3. Sidney E. Ahlstrom, *A Religious History of the American People*, Yale University Press, New Haven, p. 110ff.

NORTH CAROLINA

1. *North Carolina, The History of a Southern State*, Hugh Talmage Lefler & Albert Ray Newsome, The University of North Carolina Press, Chapel Hill, 1973, pp. 3-4.

2. Ibid., p. 7.
3. Ibid., p. 8.
4. Ibid., pp. 10-13.

NEW JERSEY

1. Corrine J. Naden, *The Colony of New Jersey*, Franklin Watts, Inc., New York, 1974, p. 1.
2. Ibid., p. 1.
3. Ibid., p. 2.
4. Ibid., p. 17.

SOUTH CAROLINA

1. Sidney E. Ahlstrom, *A Religious History of the American People*, Yale University Press, New Haven, 1977, p. 198.
2. *A History of the United States*, Vol. 1, Norman A. Graebner, Gilbert C. Fite, Phillip L. White, McGraw-Hill Book Company, New York, 1970, p. 68.
3. Sidney E. Ahlstrom, *A Religious History of the American People*, Yale University Press, New Haven, 1977, p. 197.
4. Loc. cit.
5. *A History of the United States*, Vol. 1, Norman A. Graebner, Gilbert C. Fite, Phillip L. White, McGraw-Hill Book Company, New York, 1970, p. 140.

GEORGIA

1. Marcus Wilson Jernegan, *The American Colonies 1492-1750*, Frederick Ungar Publishing Company, New York, p. 293.
2. Ibid., p. 301.

6

"And I Say to Thee: That Thou Art Peter; and upon This Rock I Will Build My Church, and the Gates of Hell Shall Not Prevail against It" (Peter [*Petros*], Rock [*Petra*], in Matthew 16:18, Douay-Rheims)

"Render therefore to Caesar the things that are Caesar's, and to God the things that are God's" (Jesus in Mark 12:17, Douay Version). "His mother Mary saith . . . Whatsoever he shall say to you, do ye" (John 2:5, Douay Version).

Jesus' words "the things that are Caesar's, and . . . the things that are God's" put state ("Caesar's") and church ("God's") into two separate categories. To put them together has always bred frustration, strife, jealousy, and a tendency to secularize faith or produce divisive movements like extreme socialism and communism. Uniting them under a governmental umbrella frightens away the gentle rain of ecumenicalism and a return to the Christianity of Jesus and the Bible.

FIVE BILLION DOLLAR INCREASE IN FEDERAL INCOME TAXES may be the next headline affecting you as an individual income tax payer. Federal budgets would be harder to balance than ever. If the federal government should allow deductions for tuition and fees at parochial and private schools, the money would have to be made up by other taxpayers, believers and unbelievers. It could quickly reach TEN BILLION. While the first year might be considerably less, for political purposes, in trying to get it started, school costs would bulge in national budgets worse than social security costs once they begin riding federal wings.

Render means to "give over" or "yield up" willingly. What America has given to everyone who lives here should inspire a nationwide effort to curtail federal spending at once. The president is wisely pointing the way thus far. . . . provided . . .

Instead of trying to drain the then abundant resources of the nation-about-to-be-born, George Washington and "the representatives of the United States of America, in General Congress"[1] pledged to the nation collectively and "to each other our Lives, our Fortunes and our sacred Honor to secure our freedoms." When Washington signed the declaration, he with others pledged the money they had ("Fortunes"). He was a millionaire at the time. They gave to declare themselves independent "from all Allegiance to the British Crown."

Every dollar we spend needlessly in the federal budget today puts the United States in jeopardy with "crowns" of the Middle East. But George Washington and his compatriots vigorously declared that any connection between them and the British crown be "totally dissolved." Pledging their "lives," "freedom," and "fortunes" cost the early fathers the risk of their lives, possessions, and honor. Dare we risk these for the luxury of supporting religious schools whose faith most do not share?

Is our religion so uninspiring or our churches so weak that they cannot survive without schools supported by the government? This does not sound like the religion of the Founding Fathers. Whose is it?

The Fathers later concluded that citizens skilled in readin', ritin', and 'rithmetic make better citizens. The government then began to require education of all.

Religion as a subject of formal instruction was and is a luxury on the curriculum of elementary and secondary schools. The homes and churches are the proper source of religious instruction —paid for by those who want it or get it.

Since when did Christianity become unable to survive without government-supported schools? Imagine Peter or Paul begging to get churches or their church schools in the budget of Nero's Rome or of the Sanhedrin's Palestine! Any religion or church (or its institutions) that cannot survive without public tax support does not deserve to survive. Original Christianity was both viable and expansive in the power of the Spirit of Christ and the Word of God. Religion too anemic to thrive in the midst of a secular milieu (or even alongside "the world, the flesh, and the devil") is inherently not viable. The sooner we see it and admit it, the better for all.

Religion is not mandatory in America. Education is. The churches and homes may assume responsibility for religion among those who want it and voluntarily accept it. But should unbelievers have it thrust upon them? Should our government compel people to support schools and religions in which they do not believe? Shall America compel them to make up for the income tax deductions allowed those who are unwilling to support their schools adequately? If they are unable, either the school is charging too much or it is a luxury item the parents can do without. Religion is in a different category from education as such. The government is not responsible for supplying it. Voluntarism alone can be the foundation of true religion.

Many religionists are beginning to assume that public schools have become dangerously secular. Is the avoidance of any semblance of sectarianism about to become "overkill" for all religion? But public schools can be basically secular without being antireligious: readin', ritin', and 'rithmetic are indispensable to Protestants, non-Protestants, and unbelievers alike.

If public schools promote antireligious ideology, parents can move toward a reasonable balance through P.T.A.s, trustees, and elected officials. Energy now focused on getting income tax deductions would be more than adequate. Parents and trustees have seldom used their maximum liberty to retain nonsectarian programs for religion in public schools on a limited and voluntary basis.

To have limited religion is neither simple nor easy. But to unload responsibility for religion from parent-trustee shoulders to those of teachers and school curriculums is a mirage. The Declaration of Independence, composed at first by Deist Thomas Jefferson, addresses Deity as "divine providence," "Supreme Judge," and "Creator" by implication in the words "created equal."

Sectarians usually are zealous for more than character, loyalty to country, and intense study to glorify the Creator. They want to go beyond the general concept of an omnipotent, omniscient, omnipresent Deity to his "genealogy" and qualify him with such philosophically contradictory phrases as "mother of God."

The Bible or Source Book of the Christian Faith addresses Deity as "Our Father" (*Pater hēmōn* in Greek Matthew 6:9), but *notre dame*, or "our mother" occurs in equal frequency in the liturgy of Roman pantheistic background. This religion of barest contact with American colonial history (see the paragraphs on Maryland in ch. four) could expect American unbelievers to support their religious schools only out of bold arrogance matching that of Pope Alexander VI of 1493 (see ch. five). The motive behind most zealous proponents for support of religious schools is sectarianism. The sect or cult flavor is remote from the simple faith of the Founding Fathers.

The Founding Fathers were religious, usually. Their faith was at least biblically oriented.

THE THINGS THAT ARE CAESAR'S

These words (Mark 12:17) refer specifically to taxes. Critics had just asked Christ, "Is it lawful to give tribute to Caesar; or shall we not give it?" (Mark 12:14, Douay Version). The Lord's answer was clear and direct: "Render therefore to Caesar the things that are Caesar's, and to God the things that are God's" (Mark 12:17, Douay Version).

His critics hoped Christ's answer would favor a tax dodge. It did not. Jesus equated support of government to good citizenship, to Christian discipleship, and to obedience to Christ as Founder of the Christian Faith (Romans 13:1ff.).

Learning to disagree agreeably is the art of gentlemen. They do not resort to nagging or becoming a nuisance every time someone disagrees with them. Efforts to crush the United States Constitution's clear legal posture against support for religious schools sometimes approach that pattern.

A fortnightly publication (March, 1981) carries the headline: "Tax Credit Parochiaid: The New Onslaught":

> The Packwood-Moynihan bill initially would divert about 1.25 billion dollars per year to parochial and private schools in the form of tuition reimbursement federal income tax credits. The credits would pay for one half of a student's tuition up to a maximum yearly benefit of $250. The maximum benefit per student per year would then rise to $500 the second year, for a total tax expenditure of $2.5 billion per year.
>
> As in 1978, the bill would also include tax credits for college and university tuition. No price tag can be put on the credits for an estimated 12 million post-secondary students because it is not known how the tax credits would interact with existing college student loan and grant programs.
>
> While the Carter Administration in 1978 came out unequivocally and strongly against tuition tax credits, the position and priorities of the Reagan Administration remain uncertain. What is certain is that Secretary of Education Terrel Bell is all in favor of tax credit parochiaid, as is his assistant secretary for planning and budget, Chester Finn, Jr., a senior aide to Moynihan who played a key role in drafting the parochiaid bill.
>
> As they did in 1977-78, Catholic parochial school interests have quietly mounted a campaign to pressure members of Congress into supporting the federal parochiaid plan.
>
> Many supporters of the newer Protestant parochial schools are holding back, largely out of fear that unwelcome federal controls on hiring and admissions would inevitably accompany the federal aid.
>
> One factor which may help to defeat the Packwood-Moynihan scheme this year is the Reagan Administration's strong drive to cut federal spending and balance the federal budget. A $2.5 billion tax expenditure for post-secondary education would flatly run counter to President Reagan's budget cutting thrust. This much was admitted by Al Senske, the Department of Education's assistant secretary for non-public education and a former official of the Lutheran Church-Missouri Synod's parochial school system. Though Senske favors parochiaid, he predicted in January that the

tax credit bill would fare poorly in Congress because "federal budget considerations" and our total economy rule it out at this point.

Some conservatives in Congress are concerned because tuition tax credits would be an "uncontrollable entitlement program." That is, once enacted, it would be an escalating drain on the federal treasury as new parochial schools are founded and old ones expand to soak up the freely hemorrhaging federal money.

Moreover, successful passage of this year's Packwood-Moynihan bill—if by some fluke it could survive a court test—would mean annual political campaigns to raise the percentage and amount of tuition reimbursed until the tax credit per student per year reached 90% or 100% of average public school costs. Even if non-public enrollment did not increase, this would mean a total annual tax expenditure of nearly $10 billion. In addition, any form of tuition tax credit aid would require establishment of a new federal bureaucracy, either in the Internal Revenue Service or the Department of Education. . . . Tuition tax credits are a tax expenditure. They would use federal tax policy to provide federal funds to sectarian private schools. The mechanism for this transaction is a federal income tax credit to reimburse parents for parochial or private school tuition. The real recipient of the federal aid is *the nonpublic school and their sponsors!* [emphasis HLE].

Tuition tax credits, thus are tax aid from all federal tax payers to that minority of religious bodies which operate private day schools. They therefore violate the First Amendment prohibition against laws "respecting establishment of religion" or laws preferring some religions over others.

The U.S. Supreme Court agrees with us on this. In PEARL v. NYQUIST (1973) and other rulings the Court has clearly held the plan unconstitutional. Senator Moynihan insists that the Court is wrong in its interpretation of the First Amendment—how else could he try to justify introducing an unconstitutional bill?—and wants the bill passed in the hope that the Supreme Court will reverse itself.[2]

The perceptive publishers and editors of the *Dallas Times Herald* editorialized, on Wednesday, March 18, 1981, on the Reagan administration's budget-trimming package and specifically on the contradictory position of the planned cut in aid to education by 25 percent while still adhering to the proposed tuition tax credit plan involving private schools. This costly tax credit program, they reasoned, though part of the Republican platform during Reagan's presidential campaign, is politically at odds with the administration's primary goal of eliminating the federal deficit. The *Times Herald*'s principal concern, however, was that the philosophy behind such a program would alter the constitutional complexion that has served the United States since its inception.

A major cause in the United States' coming into existence was absolute freedom of religion with no favoritism to any sect, cult, religion, or hybrid of the two. If even 91 percent or more of all parochial schools in the United States were owned by Rome, it would give one church only a temporary advantage. The Constitution says no as it stands. We cannot believe the Supreme Court will approve it. A more recent estimate of enrollees of parochial schools may be found on page 99.

The public schools desperately need the public. They have been the most unifying force in all of society, from many standpoints. Without them, integration will not survive. The public schools could die of lack of good teaching, mental anemia, and moral indifference if income tax deductions are available to private and religious schools.

One of the best teachers I ever had was Mrs. Nettie Gates (Presbyterian) of Lonoke, Arkansas, in the seventh and eighth grades, 1924-1926. Some students quipped intermittently, "What had she ever done to be promoted with us boys a second year!" She never bootlegged religion or quoted Scripture (she may have read it a few times). But her spirit of compassion and firm concern for us leaves her firmly ensconced in memory as one of the godliest Christians I ever knew. But I cannot remember her ever so much as calling the Lord's name in class. She did not need to. Her life, spirit, and patriotism were enough.

Later in high school football, an aggressive charging Jew played guard in front of me, a tornadic Catholic tackle, on almost every play, kept a lane open near by. A son of the local freethinker was the implacable fullback, and as a tender-footed Protestant halfback, I almost felt out of place. But at unplanned reunions, we have reminisced delightedly as fellow Americans.

Student Enrollment	Enrollment of private school students by school type*		Distribution of private schools within the United States*	
	Number	%	*Number*	%
Baptist	204,144	4.0	858	4.4
Calvinist	47,269	0.9	166	0.8
Catholic	3,269,761	64.3	9,849	50.1
Eastern Orthodox	2,682	0.1	14	0.1
Episcopal	76,452	1.5	314	1.6
Friends	14,611	0.3	50	0.3
Jewish	101,758	2.0	406	2.1
Lutheran	217,406	4.3	1,485	7.6
Methodist	11,187	0.2	60	0.3
Presbyterian	12,823	0.3	60	0.3
Seventh-day Adventist	148,157	2.9	1,106	5.6
Other Affiliations	231,317	4.5	1,351	6.7
Non-affiliated	746,730	14.7	3,944	20.1
TOTAL	5,084,297		19,663	

*Private Schools in American Education, 1976-1978 (National Center for Education Statistics, 1981).

Had each attended a different parochial school, we probably never would have met again, or in any event would have been divided Americans.

Education Secretary Terrel H. Bell, in another article in the *Dallas Times Herald,* stated that since the primary goal of the Reagan administration was to eliminate the federal deficit and reduce inflation, budget cuts were necessary and the costly tuition tax credit plan should be one of the victims of those cuts. Any other view would only cause a greater burden to local school districts.

The long sweep of history usually helps identify the educational patterns, legal principles, and legislative structures conducive to the well-being of the largest segment of society. On the basis of the assumptions in the first section of this volume, on "A Hint from History," we assume that only a long period of negative, fruitless history for the United States would warrant a change in basic legislative and legal patterns. To change to public support of religious schools would be unfair to unbelievers and partial to religions whose aggressiveness and arrogance do not reflect the need of unbelievers' money through enforced increase in income tax.

A race of American people whom business interests had imported as slaves and had subjected to literal slavery could have justified themselves in demanding legal changes (already in the Declaration of Independence in the words "created equal") that would have brought them redress. But when the redress did not come by normal processes of law, the bloodiest war of American history freed the black people, made them citizens, and in less than a century had them in a status socially and economically which they would never have acquired in their original nativity.

So much right and wrong prevailed in either direction that great and good men compromised consistently from 1829 through 1861. The Missouri Compromise almost became a territorial or geographical fad.

The War Between the States might not have occurred had the President, Zachary Taylor, lived. To persist in an issue that is either dubious, contrary to well-established principles of success as appearing in the Constitution of the United States of America, or in an issue that has spawned blood-spilling divisiveness through an enforced monolithic religious structure for the majority of European nations, hardly enhances the American spirit of *e pluribus unum*.

In the month of February, 1850, President Zachary Taylor had a difficult session with some southern gentlemen holding office in Washington. Some of them hinted at seceding from the Union. Taylor firmly stated that in order to maintain the integrity of the Union he would head an army contingent again, and pursue anyone promoting secession and "hang them with less reluctance than he had hanged deserters and spies in Mexico."[3] Had the resoluteness of Zachary Taylor been maintained throughout the nineteenth century prior to 1861, America very likely would have avoided the most gruesome war in her history. Yet the moral question of slavery and the undemocratic discrimination against a major segment of citizens were clear.

After Taylor's premature death (he was President only sixteen months), the compromisers took over and the agony of the War Between the States followed. Compromising on these kinds of issues only makes the day of reckoning harder.

Man's only hope for a God-ruled society composed of men is in the empirically undemonstrable personal, visible return of Jesus Christ. God inspired John to say of it, "Behold, he cometh with the clouds, and every eye shall see him, and they also that pierced him. And all the tribes of the earth shall bewail themselves because of him. Even so. Amen (Apoc. 1:7-8, Douay Version).

Meanwhile, theocracies headed by Saul, David, Solomon, William Penn in Massachusetts, Oliver Cromwell in England, and all the popes in Italy have failed. They have become autocracies sooner or later.

A democracy begun by thirteen colonies absolutely free of religious requirements (including government-supported religions) has succeeded. It has done better for the largest percentage of people than any government in history. Let us keep it that way, for the sake of Catholics, Protestants, and unbelievers so as to avoid having to re-enact the Protestant Reformation. What the monolithic state church in Rome has done for Europe as compared with what the loose-collared breathing room of religious pluralism has done for America and through her for the world puts the exponents of the radical change to enforced support of religious schools in an undesirable position of suspicion.

CONFUSING "CAESAR'S" WITH "GOD'S"

Does the end always justify the means? A major branch of sectarians has thrived on it. In certain areas it appears on the surface to be an absolute good. In others it becomes a ruse for eliminating dissenters and competitors. Good men would not intentionally abuse or misapply it. Ideally all things are "God's." But practically, we live in a world where we classify some things as "Caesar's." If we are wise, we recognize unbelievers and share rights with them.

The United States has tried a democracy: it works. Practically everybody, the papacy included, has tried or is trying a theocracy, and it does not work. The papacy had a thousand years (c. A.D. 565-1517) to work on it. Historians are almost unanimous in calling it the Thousand Years of Darkness. "Power corrupts. Absolute power corrupts absolutely," for imperfect human beings.

Whether Ignatius of Loyola coined the phrase, "The end justifies the means," he closely associated with it. His influence on Romanist education calls for a glimpse at his work.

Ignatius was a man of will control. In commitment to the "church," he bent his will into absolute subservience to Catholicism. He equated this altruistically to establishing the kingdom of God on earth, that is, a "theocracy."

The Saints That Moved the World describes the dramatic change of this wayward youth at about age twenty-six into a champion of will control dedicated to Catholicism. In the spring of about 1521, he knelt before a likeness of Mary in his quarters and pledged to strive as a loyal militant for Christ. His commitment had the knight-errant qualities of his chivalrous (according to that era) former life. He thereby would glorify his family and "church."[4]

The direction of his spirituality appears in his commitment to a crusade. He resolved to recapture the holy sites in the Middle East for Catholicism. The costly efforts of European Catholics to capture the Holy Land and the value of doing so (if they had succeeded) are never quite clear. The purpose probably coincides with establishing the (visible) kingdom of God in this world (theocracy), undergirding the papacy, and sustaining Holy Roman Empire ideology. The Vatican sets great store on its control of many traditional "holy" sites today.

Of special meaning is the Children's Crusades in which:

> . . . Thirty thousand French children, led by the boy Stephen, went forth under the enthusiasm of the time, they knew not whither. Multitudes died of exposure and hardship, and several thousands who secured passage to the east were seized by the Arabs and sold into slavery. A similar movement, in which twenty thousand boys and girls were involved, occurred in Germany. About five thousand reached Genoa, where they were detained. Many of these became prosperous citizens.[5]

This may have been untold suffering in one of history's greatest question marks on religion. Ignatius of Loyola may have influenced Catholic education more than any other. He epitomizes the political arm of Roman Catholicism.

Because the "church" and papacy are equivalent to God's reign on earth in much Catholic thinking, whatever one does for the "church" he does for God: thus the end justifies the means. Thus to support Catholic schools is to support the church is to support God's kingdom. Reading pp. 315-375 of the aforementioned *The Saints That Moved the World*, written strongly from the Catholic viewpoint, with its thoroughgoing historical picture of Jesuit activity, enriches one's knowledge of parochial school development in the United States.

A claim that Jesuits were in on the first well-prepared fund raising efforts for Catholic schools in the U.S.A. appears on page

371.[6] Also, the claim includes instruction of early arrivals in New York, Georgetown, Pennsylvania, Delaware, Arizona, California, as well as New and Old Mexico areas.

To exercise force or mental power over the spirits of men[7] is the end of some movements. More immediately effective than pulpiteering, the power of a church official who receives the oral divulgence of sins, they rediscovered as the perfect method for achieving permanent influence over parishioners.[8] The one confessing would regard the one receiving the confession as having authority over him. The order, according to the author of *The Saints That Moved the World,* early revived the use of this method, centering on counselling people of stature, thereby widening their power over others. If this veers near dubious methodology, the reader can scan carefully the claims for himself.[9] This is part of the historical development of one "church" school system now reaching for income tax exemption for monies paid their schools. Other Americans, unbelievers and believers, will make these deductions up by paying more income tax. Does America want to compel unbelievers thus to support the religion of Pope Alexander VI, who forbade all but those from Spain and Portugal to come to America? (See ch. three.)

The Jesuits' paramount concern in augmenting confessional activities was not for the multitudes but for the minority of strategically placed influential leaders.[10] Of even greater concern were those who would hold strategic and sensitive responsibilities in schools and government. It was an aspiration toward making those who were officially regnant in secular posts become as those commandeered by men of the cloth. The author quotes John Adams as in effect cautioning Thomas Jefferson, who followed him as president, that the followers of Loyola fill the U.S. in as many different makeups as nomads can adopt, clothed as men of many different professions. If any group deserves divine punishment here on earth and more of it hereafter, it is the followers of the founder of this order.[11] (This is the evaluation of the author of *The Saints That Moved the World,* not ours.) No greater confidence of victory ever motivated the carefully thought out methods of conquering the ruling body of ancient Rome.

The Carrolls kept Jesuits out of Maryland for years so as not to frighten away badly needed Protestant settlers. When they were admitted, the nobleman of Maryland kept the Jesuits from circumscribing the Protestants.[12]

A primary source of colonial days records that interspersed with the various Protestant groups were numerous clandestine papal representatives of Loyola's order. (See *America Before the Revolution 1725-1775*, A. T. Vaughn, Prentice Hall, Inc., New Jersey, p. 109.)

WORLDWIDE RELIGIONS

No less than seven major religions survive vigorously. They are Confuscianism, Buddhism, Shintoism, Islam, Judaism, Roman Catholicism, and evangelical Christianity. Contemporary Roman Catholicism is a great social-minded, universally postured, ecclesiastically directed faith, but it long since decisively left Christianity as evidenced in its hierology, teleology, and theology.

This does not mean that Roman Catholics cannot be saved. The Syrophenician woman in Mark 7:26 saw beyond Christ's garment to Christ himself and was made whole as she touched his garment. Many men, women, and youth, both Protestant and Catholic, often see beyond what they have been mistaught to Jesus himself, who alone can save them (Romans 1:16-17, 3:1-17).

A. HIEROLOGY

Hierology includes the history and lore of a religion. *Alone of All Her Sex*, an attractive, accurate representation of the Catholic viewpoint, is in chapter three, herein, entitled "Mary beyond Scripture." Its consideration leads to a fairer and richer appraisal of both doctrinal and social postures.

In the origin of Roman Catholicism, Constantine (a non-Christian Roman ruler about A.D. 311-312), deadlocked in military struggle with Maxentius, claimed to have had a vision of a cross in the sky accompanied by the words, "By this conquer."[13] The rising popularity of Christianity, together with the plausibility of the vision, apparently brought spirit to his soldiers. He soundly defeated Maxentius at the Milvian Bridge just outside Rome marching under the banner of the cross. One of Constantine's titles was Pontifex Maximus; now it means a bishop or pope. *This papal title thus came from a Roman emperor.* The moral standard of the emperor's subsequent life hardly measured up to elementary Christianity. The title still refers to both. That is, the office is still an appendage of a state! It combines the structure of the Roman Empire with the ancient pantheistic pattern of the lore and cultism of ancient Roman religions. Constantine admired the cohesive brotherliness of Christians as potent for cementing his crumbling Empire.

Constantine immediately became very partial to Christians. Pagan rituals and rites offensive to Christians were stifled and the clergy were exempted from taxes and military service. He established Sunday for civil observance. "In 324 A.D. he was said to have promised to every convert to Christianity twenty pieces of gold and a white baptismal robe. Twelve thousand men, with women and children in proportion, were said to have been baptized in Rome in one year. The persistent adherence of the Roman aristocracy to paganism was a matter of great concern to Constantine, and he took special pains to overcome the antipathy of the Romans toward Christianity."[14] In 325, he formally asked all citizens to accept the faith. He was a missionary of sorts, but his methods paved the way for the Dark Ages. Practically, but not officially, the faith now enjoyed the status of a state religion. Many from other Roman religions came into Christianity without basic knowledge of Christ. Leaders changed the faith rapidly. Even priests from cults in the Roman Empire came into the churches untaught. This is not the religion that left Jerusalem (c. A.D. 35-45) or Antioch (Acts 13:1-4, c. A.D. 46 to A.D. 63).

The Roman pantheon is a fascinating study of the many religions of the past based on man's striving to find and know God. Meanwhile the Christian revelation carries the assurance of what ultimate reality is like: "I am the way, and the truth, and the life.

No man cometh to the Father, but by me . . . he that seeth me seeth the Father also" (John 14:6, 9, Douay Version). Also, "Jesus Christ is the same yesterday and today, yes, and forever" (Hebrews 13:8, Douay Version). "For in him dwelleth all the fulness of the Godhead corporeally [bodily]" (Col. 2:9, Douay Version). This means no aspect of God changes. Nor do humans become deities. Christians do not claim to be perfect people but imperfect disciples serving and studying a perfect Savior.

The proliferation of literature and ritual from the Roman cults began to dilute the pristine Christianity from Antioch (Acts 11:26, 13:1-3) and Jerusalem (Acts 1:8). As Constantine saw the cohesive power of early Christian brotherhood and love, he yearned to have them permeate his crumbling empire. When Romans [at first] refused to accept the new religion, Constantine transferred his capital to Byzantium and built Constantinople, or New Rome.

The written record of the Judeo-Christian revelation accompanied the real movement—the Bible. This is what made the difference between Christianity and ultimate Romanism. Paul's letter to the Romans was early enough to reflect the mutuality of doctrinal agreement with pure evangelical Christianity at that time (A.D. 57-58).

Elton Trueblood's observation shows the role of the Bible appropriate to any date.

> As we gain a clearer historical understanding of the development of religious experience we are helped to see that the contrast between reason and revelation may be more a matter of object than of method. The main claim of revelation is not that the human recipient is made aware, by a special method, of a set of truths about God, but the far more exciting claim that he is made aware of God Himself. This was a point on which Archbishop Temple helped many minds, especially when he dealt with the relationship between what man can learn by observation and what he can learn by revelation. The essence of revelation, he taught, "is intercourse of mind and event, not the communication of doctrine distilled from that intercourse." God may, indeed, break into a man's life as He did into the life of Job, but He does not, for that reason, relieve Job or any other man of the necessity of working out, by careful analysis,

his own answer to the problem of evil. . . . The revelation, if it comes, is a religious experience rather than a merely intellectual one, and it requires for its full understanding the addition of thought quite as much as does any other experience. The major reason for this requirement is that a supposed revelation may be a false one. Since there are several alleged revelations, many of which are strictly incompatible with one another, they cannot all be genuine. What about the supposed revelation to Joseph Smith? Both he and his immediate followers felt that this revelation was as genuine and as important as that of the Old or the New Testament. Was he right? Were the gold plates really there? As soon as we try to answer this question we are already out of the area of revelation and well embarked in the area of reason, because we are forced to apply tests of credibility, and they are highly complex. In short, revelation is not self-validating! We must always ask the question of why it is reasonable to believe that a revelation has occurred. We have gained greatly from the widespread application of the historical method, so that we know something of the steps by which the alleged revelations have come about. The Bible may, indeed, be God's direct revelation to finite men, but it is our philosophical duty to ask how we know that this is true.

The important conclusion here is that the appeal to revelation is not and cannot be a final appeal, because if it were, every fanatic would be justified in his uncritical assertions. If we are told that the mother of Jesus was perpetually a virgin, we have a right to ask the nature of the evidence. Was it revealed? Then to whom? Certainly, it does not appear in the Biblical account, where reference is made to the brothers of Christ [Mark 6:3]. The claim may be a justifiable claim, but it needs careful substantiation. It is not true just because somebody says so.

The necessary conclusion is that reason and revelation, far from being incompatible, need to go together at all times. If reason is required to leave out all reference to revelation, it has no religious experience, for example, as the heart of the empirical evidence for the reality of God. The best evidence is the evidence which is in the Bible, the very book which in the past has been looked upon as the special preserve of revealed religion. If, on the other hand, revelation is espoused without the critical examination which reason provides, we have no guarantee against superstition and ecclesiastical pretension.[15]

Catholicism was in the process of strong consolidation by the mid-fifth century. By A.D. 451, Emperor Valentinian III was subservient to Leo, the bishop of the church in Rome. When Anatolius, patriarch of Constantinople, proceeded to use his right "to ordain the metropolitans,"[16] Leo excommunicated him. The emperor compelled Anatolius to give in. As a result, the primacy of Rome, long an ambition of many, became a reality. Her bishop was in effect "the bishop of bishops,"[17] with the Council of Chalcedon in effect approving (A.D. 451). The Roman church, located in the capital of the empire, grew in numbers, wealth, prestige, and, above all, in organizational efficiency. While eastern churches bogged down in doctrinal controversies, Rome was practical and zealously missionary. The crystallizing of its centrality in A.D. 451 set the pattern in a context of wealth, political machinations, and organic union with the state for centuries.[18]

With the "church" ruled by the same person who controlled the Roman Empire, further consolidation was simple and rapid. The same individual held both positions. Leo may have been first to try this (A.D. 450-451). Thus the papacy and foundation for the Holy Roman Empire came simultaneously. "The State spiritual is thenceforth to be represented as fully and as universally by the bishop of Rome as the State temporal is represented by the emperor."[19] But the church and state cannot function coterminously and simultaneously as both entities. It may be one unit or the other but not both. It may 'play church' and say "te absolvo" to the naive as though to forgive sins for God. Or it may 'play state' to the Supreme Court and say, "Support our Catholic schools like we tell you." But thinking minds, seeing what the American way has done, won't fall for that. It is either a church or a state but it is not both. This is one of the most penetrating statements by a responsible historian on how church and state came to be fused in early minds to keep the advantages of both church and empire in "union"; its contemporary contradictory form and activity help keep the "parody" alive. The claims to absolute theocracy in Rome today appear in (1) papal infallibility and in (2) papal authority which are no less than effort at an autocracy. It would thus bleed America both ways.

Pope Gregory the Great (A.D. 590-604) simply tightened papal supremacy and projected Catholic missions. He projected missionary representatives to Britain and Germany where simple evangelical patterns of Christianity had long prevailed. He would have subjected these Christians to the Roman See (the bishop of Rome). He extended the authority of the Roman See by such aggressive missions (actually compulsive monolithic forms of worship) to unify the pantheism of the Empire (whose centrifugal force naturally tended toward heterogeneity) and by forming advantageous treaty agreements with civil rulers. He climaxed all this by insisting on uniformity of worship throughout Christendom. The Roman Empire's official embracing of Christianity and giving it established status clearly was to unite the empire and avert its crumbling apart. Christianity probably spread to Britain through the Roman army by the end of the second century. By A.D. 600, Iro-Scottish Celts were zealously missionary and were spreading the faith among people in France, Germany, and in northern Britain.

B. THEOLOGY

Has Roman Catholicism been removed from the Christianity of Jesus and His apostles (including Peter—II Peter 3:15-16)? This issue is inherent first in the word *grace*. In "grace," biblical Christianity's contrast with other religions leaves them at opposite poles.

Bible students often define *grace* as "undeserved favor." But this is too delicate. Grace is not passive, it is dynamic and aggressive. It is that aspect of the love of God in His absolute being that pursues man vigorously until He either wins man or the man says no to Him with finality.

Several attributes, without which grace is not grace, put it in sharp focus. First, "But to him that worketh not, yet believeth in him that justifieth the ungodly, his faith is reputed to justice, according to the purpose of the grace of God" (Rom. 4:5, Douay Version).

God bestows His grace directly and only through the Holy Spirit. It is a question of logistics. This military term has often made the difference between winning and losing a battle. So with grace. God transports and applies His grace to sinful men through the Holy Spirit only (see John 16:7-15; Rom. 8:1-16; II Peter 1:2) and not through men. Men, including priests, can deliver only information and testimony, like any other Christian.

Man delivered grace, so-called, only frustrates or defeats the divine-human encounter. Men cannot deliver grace. It must be Holy Spirit delivered grace and not bellhop delivered grace. As God's Spirit brings it and ministers it to the seeking soul, the believer then experiences Christ in salvation. But red-cap delivered grace reminds him of a man and the institution he represents to which he is now indebted, presumably.

Blaise Pascal (1623-1662) had not had the religious instruction specifically that would have led him to experience Christ. But the thinking of Pascal (one of the world's greatest mathematicians) was so accurate that he arrived at genuine evangelical religion and spiritual experience. His thoughts are stimulating both devotionally and intellectually.[20] He never left the Catholic state church but was a strong believer in Christ and the logical processes of biblical spirituality. He is a favorite Catholic thinker. Pascal claimed personal and experiential religion in his relationship to God in Christ.

THE FREE MIND: ARTS AND SCIENCES

Other fields have elicited high performance as shackles of thought control and institutionalism have given way to reality. Roman Catholic Lecomte du Nouy was a famous mathematician of France. His chief work, which first influenced us deeply in 1949-50, is entitled *Human Destiny* (translation published by the New American Liberty, New York).

The distinct contributions of du Nouy were (1) his mathematical demonstrations that the universe could not have happened by chance, and (2) that the human being created in the image of the Creator and Sustainer of the universe is obligated to be his best morally and ethically. This incited him as it did the aforementioned mathematician, Blaise Pascal, to seek his way at least into the vestibule of some profound evangelical truths. He may not have come all the way. He never left the Catholic fold. But the effective manner in which he thought and articulated his thinking makes him helpful to many believers. Pascal's *Pensees* are intellectually invigorating and devotionally inspiring.

The Catholic poet, Joyce Kilmer, in two lines of his "Trees" reached almost the same lofty note:

> *Poems are made by fools like me,*
> *But only God can make a tree.*

We read that Kilmer once was hovering between life and death as he lay on the edge of a field of battle. The changing sun caused a nearby tree to cast a shadow over his parching face. From this came the inspiration for "Trees," according to this account. An experience that opens the vistas of eternity to a tired and outreaching soul can come to one who at the time is thinking in the vestibule of eternal reality. God in Christ can indeed satisfy him then. See Christ's exaltation and humiliation in Philippians 2:5-11, where His lordship is not to be impinged upon by anyone. (*By Life or by Death,* same author, Exposition Press, pp. 60-72.)

PETROS AND PETRA

The church is a major doctrine, not marginal. It embraces the entire field of ecclesiology (from Greek *eklesia* or church, in turn from *kaleo* which, prefaced with *ek,* "from" or "out," means "to call out"). The true church consists of the "called out ones," who must voluntarily and responsibly obey the call. By no means are they to be inducted in infancy (Eph. 1:18-20).

The first mentioned objective of the church is sharing the good news as seen in "keys": ". . . and upon this rock I will build my church; and the gates of hell shall not prevail against it. And I will give unto thee the keys of the kingdom of heaven . . ." (Matt. 16:18-19, Douay Version). When Jesus said to Peter and the apostles, "Thou art Peter" (*petros*), He used Peter's name because he was the only disciple whose name made a pun with the word *petra*, or "rock."

Petra appears in Isaiah 16:1 from Hebrew *Sela*: "Send forth, O Lord, the lamb, the ruler of the earth, from Petra of the desert, to the mount of the daughter of Sion" (Douay Version).

Sela is the Hebrew word for the all-rock city of Petra carved into a mammoth mountain of rock. It is sixteen miles south of the Dead Sea in Jordan. The city and its buildings may be over a mile long and scores of yards thick and high in places, of solid, carved rock.

Petra had been in existence and well known since at least the year 300 B.C. Developed by the Nabataeans, these ancients had carved government buildings, a treasury house, living and market facilities, back into the rock. Soon after the Romans took it over in the first century, it had a Roman aqueduct for water and drainage of sewage, all of pure rock.

The Douay Version is one of the few correct translations. Some King James Version editions transliterate *Sela* and print a footnote indicating it is Petra, using capital *s* and *p* respectively. Thus they knew of the same rock city and its Greek name in the first century or earlier. *Petra* is the Greek word translated from *Sela* in Isaiah 16-1: A *petra* or *sela* may have large strata and other stone entities, but it appears essentially as one continuing piece of stone.

Thus the "Keys of the kingdom" are for all disciples (Matt. 16:19). Jesus vigorously declared a "key" to be "knowledge" in Luke 11:52. This is the knowledge of Christ as Messiah and Son of God, which Peter had just confessed. Every time a Christian shares this with another he is using the key of knowledge of Christ's Deity and Messiahship to unlock men's hearts.

DEMOCRATIC, AUTOCRATIC, OR
THEOCRATIC CHURCH?

The dictatorship of one man or a small group of men over the church reverses the teaching of Christ. The first crisis the church had was over this. The Judaizers tried to compel all Christians to accept circumcision and to keep the law of Moses. Is salvation through Christ alone or through Christ plus some ritual or rite like circumcision? After much debate, the church itself decided. Not merely part of the church or the officials of the church, but "the whole church" (Acts 15:22) made the decision. The Douay Version translates with precisely the same words as the King James Version, namely "with the whole church," in Acts 15:22.

And Peter was there (Acts 15:7). He testified (Acts 15:7-11) and then voted as James presided (Acts 15:7-11, Douay Version)! The church is healthier, stronger, and more aggressive when it is free and democratic.

No pope has ever come to America with a smile of contrition on his face and an apology on his lips, emanating from his heart, about the people burned at the stake for dissenting back in the 15th and 16th centuries. No apology has ever come for the way dissenters were driven out of Europe by the state church leadership and forced to come to the wilderness of America. All are strangely oblivious to Jesus' words in Matthew 5:23.

Also, enforced sharing of a nation's wealth has resulted largely from "established" or government-supported religion. "Established" churches ultimately have too much financial control.

The incentive for this statement comes from Catholic Lord Acton. "Lord Acton believed that the ideal state in the development of historical science would be reached when the life of Martin Luther would be substantially the same whether written by a Protestant or a Roman Catholic. Some scholars now approximate this idea."[21]

We would add that not all of the Reformation tension was theological. Luther was a great theologian. However, at points he was very inconsistent. For a man who gave wings to the slogan

Sola Scriptura, his "consubstantiation" is hardly more than a compromise with the unreasonable literalistic interpretation of John 6:53 that the "priest" miraculously turns the bread and wine into the literal flesh and blood of Christ (transubstantiation).

Martin Luther was a great man by any standard. When one realizes the dangers of death (burning at the stake), and the personal humiliation of being declared unorthodox by his brethren, he was indeed a man of almost incomparable courage. Even a prominent denominational committee can label a man as "too liberal" or "too conservative" and try to give him a devastating image.

The princes and others were quick to take advantage of the theological reformation to secure some reforms in land division. They secured them. Their action may have postponed communism from 1517 to October 1917. The church had such great holdings of land and other wealth that the case for communism seemed exceedingly plausible to many. Some did not bother with the theology. Church officials owned half of Bohemia as members of the church hierarchy burned John Huss at the stake, July 6, 1415 (Encyclopaedia Britannica, Vol. II, p. 910).[22]

The problems of land and wealth division have plagued the Catholic countries and other non-evangelical countries more than any other nations in the world, from Cuba to China. Percentage-wise, the largest Communist vote cast regularly, outside Russia, for decades has been the Communist vote in Italy, which presumably is at least mildly Catholic. Cuba, Mexico, and countries in South America would have gone Communist earlier but for the aid they received from evangelical United States.

Lord Acton was correct, and this may be one application of his principle. His full name was Lord John Emerich Edward Dalberg Acton, or the first Baron 8th Baronette Acton.

We asked a friend recently, "Do you think the United States should have a Catholic president?" Pensively and philosophically he finally said, "Yes, I think I've devised a set of criteria for it. Every time Ireland elects an Anglican head of state, every time Spain places a Presbyterian in its top political position, every time

Italy elects a Pentecostal prime minister, I think in view of the history of the United States and Europe, if a Catholic candidate qualifies, we should elect him president."

C. TELEOLOGY

State aid, empire, and ecclesiasticism merge in a state-church. Romanism aspires to "rule," beginning in countries where it has "churches." This is partially the purpose in requiring the state to support the church or its institutions whether the people believe in its theology or not. This is comparable, in essence, to the Holy Roman Empire, which was coextensive with the Thousand Years of Darkness.

This penchant for ruling appears in the two bulls issued by the pope in 1493 (see chs. four and five under "Rejecting Mary's Advice"). Pope Alexander VI ruled that only countries under his sphere of influence could enter the western hemisphere. Most of us living in America now he forbade to come! Every non-Catholic living in America today does so in defiance of a papal order, which has never been cancelled as far as we know. Seldom ever is an open action more revelatory of the Vatican ends. The present pope is Alexander's successor. He is likely a godly man according to Roman Catholicism. We lament his misfortunes of May 13, 1981, have prayed for his recovery, but the institution and its goals are immutable.

The logistics concerning the sacraments undergird this power method. Assuming them to be seven, only the priest is to administer the sacraments, save in emergencies. Thus again this office (priest), which does not even exist as such in New Testament Christianity (The Apocalypse 1:5; Ephesians 2:20, Douay Version), is the means for dispensing grace.

THE THINGS THAT ARE GOD'S

Christ taught that grace is solely the work of the Holy Spirit in the individual (see John 16:7-16 and Rom. 8:9-17). Red-cap delivered grace is not the divine, saving, keeping grace of the Christian revelation (see especially Eph. 2:8-9). Such man-delivered grace has institutionalized the "church" beyond all recognition. The revelation that left Jerusalem and Antioch hardly took rest in Rome until the Roman pantheon drew out its life as Constantine and successors fastened it on to keep the Empire from crumbling. Every communicant will discover that only God's grace, Spirit-delivered, works "in the hour of our death." It ties the communicant to God and not to the state church. So once again, the true teleological objective of the "church" is not to rule and control as did the Roman Empire, but to reign through God's Spirit in people to produce brotherliness.

Christian love alone is the hallmark of Christianity: "By this shall all men know that you are my disciples, if you have love one for another" (John 13:35, Douay Version).

Another graham cracker plank in the foundation of a hierarchical system shows up in compulsory celibacy. Christ put celibacy strictly on a voluntary basis for any man: "For there are eunuchs, who were born so from their mother's womb: and there are eunuchs, who were made so by men: and there are eunuchs, who have made themselves eunuchs for the kingdom of heaven. He that can take, let him take" (Matt. 19:12, Douay Version; see ch. three).

Organizational structure represents the actual heart and mind. If a religious body is more like the structure of the Roman Empire than it is like the Lord's church, it is not the heart and mind of Christ. He said, "Ye know that they who seem to rule over the Gentiles lord it over them: and their princes have power over them. But it is not so among you: but whosoever will be greater shall be your servant" (Mark 10:42-43, Douay Version). A hierarchy is the opposite to the Christian pattern.

The Vatican is both a state and a church. The priest who represents the church also represents the state.

For it (the church-state) to deal with a government (the U. S.), it is taking advantage of the government because it (the U. S. Government) is benign beyond compare to all churches, even to the point of naivete.

America's early experience with churches came when the main product of churches was people striving for a purer pattern of life. Their goal was not to see how much money they could bleed from the state or how many concessions they could eke out of government at all levels. Those churches simply strove to produce good people.

This church-state drove many of United States' original settlers to these wildernesses between 1492 and 1789. How this church-state could now ask for favors and concessions is beyond all bounds of Christian propriety and elementary courtesy. What changed it from persecuting bloodily to suddenly courting the government whose Declaration of Independence only *one* Roman Catholic signed? (See first paragraph on Maryland in ch. four).

FOUR ATTACKS ON AMERICAN LIBERTIES

The four famous attacks on American freedom are (1) the class system, (2) racial discrimination, (3) the assumption that one sex is inferior to the other, and now (4) the ecclesiastical encroachment.

The earliest attack was the seignorial system, based on lords, counts, dukes, earls, etc., as inherited titles of privilege. A fortune usually went with the title. This antiquated system died aborning in the rugged frontier life of America. The United States has no lords, counts, dukes, earls—or kings—only cardinals who are potential popes or ecclesiastical kings.

The second attack was racially and economically grounded. It caused the unfortunate episode of American slavery. It was an inequity based on the assumption that one man could own another. Lamentably, color or skin pigmentation was the chief criterion on which this inequity subsisted. In a young nation inbred with the ideology of democracy and in considerable measure committed to New Testament theology, the idea that one man could possess another was an un-Christian reversion to the heathen patterns of the Greco-Roman world. It was not unusual for a Roman to own one or more slaves.

The United States settled the race issue in legal theory by the War Between the States (1861-1865). We still have much progress to make in practicing the brotherhood we have professed. It was in the Declaration of Independence all along in the words "created equal."

The third attack on elementary American liberty was the effort to attribute to women a *second-rate status*. On August 26, 1920, the State Department announced that thirty-six state legislatures had ratified the 19th Amendment and that it was from that date accordingly a part of the Constitution of the United States. No citizen's right to vote can be abridged by gender, legally, since that date.

The fourth is the ecclesiastical attack. It assumes that one man can affect another man's destiny or status in life after death. It presumes that he has an inside track to the Source of forgiveness. *Te absolvo*, or "I forgive you," are not words for any man. "But God only" can forgive sins, which Christ the Son shared with the Father (Mark 2:10, Douay Version).

A priest and a church hierarchy seriously claim power to forgive sins, to shorten or prolong the punishment for sins in the afterlife. This has been known to control men's decisions in this world. One author states this is the reason Ignatius of Loyola led his order early to adopt oral confession, namely that it magnifies ecclesiastics' power over communicants' lives (see *The Saints That Moved the World,* pp. 357, 358, 363, 370, 373).

This attack is usually led by church officials filling an office that never existed in New Testament churches (Mark 15:38 and Eph. 2:20). At the death of Christ, when the fifty-foot-long veil in the temple before the mercy seat was rent in twain "from the top to the bottom" (Mark 15:38), the need for priests died and the office as such died. Any man can enter the Holy of Holies it covered—alone—and negotiate with his Maker by himself. You search the Bible in vain for a priest who ever held this office as such in a Christian church, save as all Christians are priests metaphorically and spiritually: "And hath made us a kingdom, and priests to God and his Father, to him be glory and empire forever and ever. Amen" (Apoc. 1:6, Douay Version).

A priesthood that now claims to be able to forgive the sins of parishioners, a priest who is able to shorten the stay of a communicant or one of his loved ones in "purgatory," has a life-hold upon him. Unthinking people ask his advice or take his suggestion regarding practically everything, from whom or what to vote for to suggestions concerning socialism, government, and ethics.

One spiritual giant said in 1921, "But what of America in this great program? The eyes of all the world are on America. Emerson said that America seems to have been the last effort of Divine Providence in behalf of the race. The Hon. Mr. Bryce, the Honourable Ambassador of Great Britain, said that America is attempting the largest experiment in self-government in the history of the world. And the noble Spurgeon said to one of our American brethren a little before his departure, 'Go back to your country and tell your men that the hopes of the world are centered in your country—the free church in the free State—and do your best.' "[24]

In typical timeliness he added, "Thrilling was the scene in 1870, when in the Vatican the dogma of papal infallibility was passed. In the awful excitement and clamour of that hour, Archbishop Manning, later Cardinal Manning, sought to quell the tremendous agitation of his fellow ecclesiastics. When he got their attention, holding in his hand the paper pronouncing papal infallibility as the doctrine of Romanists—holding that dogma in his hands—he said, 'Let all the world go to bits and we Catholics will reconstruct it on this paper.' What has the evangelical Christian to say when he hears that? Taking up a little book and holding it aloft, his word to the world is, 'Let all the world go to bits and we will reconstruct it on the authority of Jesus Christ as voiced in this New Testament.' Some things in this world are unchangeably true and others are just as unchangeably false, and never did truth win her battles on any land or in the midst of any people by compromising the truth. Oh . . . we long for the union of God's people; but we want no omnibus compromise; we want no sham union or unity; we want union and unity alone on the authority of the Son of God."[25]

Satanic forces use the hassle of liberalism and conservatism (so-called) as an albatross to take believers' minds off the real issue. Exponents of sacramentarianism (proxy religion and man-delivered grace) never let up in their efforts to get tax support. The real issues are (1) Will Americans cling to the personalized experiential faith of the Founding Fathers? and (2) Will she refuse any subtle device that places religion largely outside the pale of voluntarism by supporting schools which "require" religion? Distinctive American liberty would die, if we give in.

To ask for direct or indirect tax aid to parochial schools is a betrayal of the only Roman Catholic who signed the Declaration of Independence. The noble Charles Carroll of Carrollton even agreed to an American-selected hierarchy. This would have avoided the complication of church "rulers" selected by other nationals to control the lives of American Catholics.

Religious schools by biblically oriented Christian churches can be an asset, provided they pay their own way. They are costly, usually prohibitive to churches: we tried one, grades one through six, from 1948 to 1954. The *Dallas Morning News* (January 8, 1982, p. 15A) reported a $2.5 million gift for the academy of the church pastored by Dr. W. A. Criswell in Dallas, Texas. This may be one of Dr. Criswell's greatest accomplishments. Such schools can demonstrate their worthwhileness and justify their cost by the character and ability they generate in their constituents. Meticulous records can be kept over a sufficient period of time to verify the facts one way or the other. But schools are expensive. When money is available, try them, even on a citywide or group basis. Otherwise stay out of them. Religious schools will seldom have adequate support even if they had volunteer teachers from religious orders.

Certain philosophies and sectarian theology can legally be in the curriculums of church schools. Many Protestants admit that the Reformation is still unfinished. The Reformers barely began it. We can best continue it in the United States. America has supplied the best milieu for its implementation. Protestants have the Bible. But they must use it—in everything from social problems to church organization and doctrine. It alone should be the determinative factor regarding ritual, rites, and order of service.

Cannot the church survive without the Bible? That is precisely what Luther in 1517 was "protesting" against—a church without the Bible.

The Roman capital and ruling class "received" the Christian faith on the condition they could reign over it (A.D. 12-24). When Christianity first made its way into the city of the Caesars, it entered by alleys and lived in cellars. But as Constantine began to merge church and state, a pope soon emerged wearing the crown of a Caesar. Later Pope Gregory (Hildebrand) would require Emperor Henry to do penance by standing in the snow with his bare feet at Canossa, and he wrote his famous letter to William the Conqueror to the effect that the state was subordinate to the church, that the power of the state as compared to the church was "as the moon compared to the sun."[26] From Constantine to Pope Alexander VI of *bulla* fame, limiting the western hemisphere to two Catholic countries;[27] from Pope John XXIII of "ecumenical" gestures to Pope John Paul—all these personalities have functioned on the "traditional" conditions of genuflexes, financial support for church schools wherever obtainable, Vatican ambassadorial favors to put them above all others, and honoring a pope's ring in obeisance. From and through all these the papacy, its orders, and its personnel have operated as an empire and not as a Spirit-filled church.

Contrast Rome's conditions of acceptance of Christianity with the spirit of other equally qualified rulers.

After her demise, as well as while she lived, many startling incidents came out regarding England's world-famed queen, Victoria. When the time came, while she was yet a girl, for her to be crowned queen of England, it was arranged that the climax of the coronation exercises should be the singing of Handel's Messiah. "The young queen had been reared in modest seclusion, and therefore did not understand the dignified ways of the court. And so she was informed by the court ladies that though everyone else should rise during the singing of that great oratorio, she must not rise, it would not be proper for royalty, her position was too dignified. The exercises began and went on until the concluding moments, when the great oratorio should be sung, and the sublime strains swept on, thrilling every heart. 'He shall reign forever and forever.' At those words the young queen was seen to tremble with deep emotion, but according to instructions she did not rise. The singers reached those words: 'King of kings and Lord of lords, King of kings and Lord of lords.' The young queen could no longer remain seated, she rose, lifted her eyes heavenward, then bowed her head and wept."[28]

A faith that lays the crowns of men at the feet of the King of kings settled in the early colonies of America. Theirs was not a religion of grasping for diadems, sceptres, and kissing royal rings for themselves. They wrote a constitution that called for democracy, not autocracy and theocracy. This God-inspired democracy provides luxury, liberty, and opportunity for most of us today, if we in faith and courage will take it.

"There were more than 3 million and possibly less than 3½ million people in the original thirteen colonies in 1776 and only 22,000 were non-Protestant Christians." The *Democratic Experience* states that the population of the United States in 1800 was 5,308,433 (p. 374).

The ratio 22,000:5,308,433 shows the number of Catholic communicants relative to the total population in about 1776, before and after. Is this about .5 of 1 percent? This was the approximate relationship near the founding of the United States. Is this about one-half of 1 percent for the "state-church communicants" and 99 5/10 percent for nonbelievers and Protestants? What is the record of the religious tradition when they have secured government support to any degree for their schools? Has it ever founded a democratic nation?

"We, the people," can resolve this issue under God in the spirit of American brotherliness.

Notes

1. *The Encyclopedia Americana International Edition*, Vol. 8, Americana Corporation, 575 Lexington Avenue, New York, p. 591.

2. "Tax Credit Parochiaid: The New Onslaught" in Church & State, Vol. 34, No. 3, 8120 Fenton Street, Silver Springs, Maryland, March 1981, p. 3ff.

3. Frank Freidel, *Our Country's Presidents*, National Geographic Society, Washington, D.C., 1975, p. 83.

4. Rene Fulop-Miller, *The Saints That Moved the World*, Collier Books, New York, 1965, p. 315-375, 323.

5. Albert Henry Newman, *A Manual of Church History*, Vol. 1, American Baptist Publication Society, Philadelphia, 1904, p. 461.

6. Rene Fulop-Miller, *The Saints That Moved the World*, Collier Books, New York, 1965, p. 371.

7. Loc. cit., p. 358-365.

8. Loc. cit., p. 357.

9. Ibid.

10. Ibid.

11. Loc. cit., p. 374.

12. *The Democratic Experience*, Degler, Cochran, De Santis, Hamilton, Harbaugh; Scott, Foresman, and Company, Glenview, Illinois, 1973, p. 15.

13. Albert Henry Newman, *A Manual of Church History*, Vol. 1, American Baptist Publication Society, Philadelphia, 1904, p. 306.

14. Ibid.

15. David Elton Trueblood, *Philosophy of Religion*, Harper & Row Publishers, New York, 1957, p. 29f.

16. Albert Henry Newman, *A Manual of Church History*, Vol. 1, The American Baptist Publication Society, Philadelphia, 1904, p. 399.

17. Loc. cit., p. 391.

18. Loc. cit., p. 399.

19. Loc. cit., p. 398.

20. Blaise Pascal, *Pascal's Pensees*, E.P. Dutton Publishers, New York, 1958.

21. David Elton Trueblood, *Philosophy of Religion,* Harper & Row Publishers, New York, 1957, pp. 44f.

22. F. L. Cross, Ed., *The Oxford Dictionary of the Christian Church,* Oxford University Press, London, p. 679.

23. George W. Truett, *God's Call to America,* Sunday School Board of Southern Baptist Convention, Nashville, Tennessee, p. 26.

24. Ibid., p. 12.

25. Ibid., p. 21.

26. Ibid., p. 25.

27. Ibid., p. 46.

28. Ibid., p. 138.